Between Faith and History
A BIOGRAPHY OF
J. A. KUFUOR

By Ivor Agyeman-Duah

Africa World Press, Inc.

P.O. Box 1892
Trenton, NJ 08607

P.O. Box 48
Asmara, ERITREA

Africa World Press, Inc.

P.O. Box 1892
Trenton, NJ 08607

P.O. Box 48
Asmara, ERITREA

Book and cover design: Roger Dormann

Library of Congress Cataloging-in-Publication Data

Agyeman-Duah, Ivor, 1966-
Between faith and history : a biography of J.A. Kufuor /
  by Ivor Agyeman-Duah.
      p. cm.
ISBN 1-59221-128-3 (hardcover) — ISBN 1-59221-129-1 (pbk.)
  1. Kufuor, John Agyekum, 1938- 2. Presidents—Ghana—
Biography. 3.
Ghana—Politics and government—1979- I. Title.

  DT512.34.K84A34 2003
  966.705—dc21

                                    2003012034

Dedication

In the course of writing this book, I had my first child—Nana Akwasi Agyeman-Duah, who I have named for my late father—Joseph Agyeman-Duah. My hope for him and children born of his generation is that, the Ghana that they will finally inherit will be one that will make them proud of the efforts and achievements of their forefathers.

Acknowledgements

Memories always shared become stories to be told from one generation to another. This in essence is a collective memory given out. I will like to thank in particular His Excellency J.A. Kufuor for access to him over the years and more important for giving me the independence to tell a story in which he was and is still a major player. Nana Akua Durowaa or Agnes Addo Kufuor, the lead family historian from Apagyafie, was most insightful during the research and showed such clarity of understanding. Since I was a very young boy, I have listened to her tell me many historical incidents from the 1700s as narrated to her. Her attention to details and her sharp memory even in her late seventies has served me well.

Other leading informants included Dr. Kwame Addo Kufuor, the Apagyahene Oheneba Osei Kyeretwie, Nana Ama Kufuor and many other non-family members.

I am also grateful to Professor David Owusu Ansah of James Madison University, who first read the manuscript and gave it a good commendation as well as making very useful suggestions. Dr. Lawrence Mbogoni of William Paterson University in New Jersey, Prof. Emmanuel Akyeampong of Harvard University and Dr. Kofi Ellison of the U.S. Justice Department, Washington, DC all read the manuscript at different stages.

Gratitude also go to Roberta Maldima and Doreen Ackom of the Ghana Embassy in Washington, DC, Joe Amoako Adusei and Bismarck Badu of *West Africa* magazine.

As we say, the shortfalls are mine.

Contents

Foreword

A good biography reveals not only the life of its subject but also the times in which the person lived. If the biography is of a politician, the book should encompass insights into the politics of the era. Ivor Agyeman-Duah's book about President J.A. Kufuor achieves that fusion of narrative between the biography of a man and the history of a country.

In writing this Foreword I in turn had to strike a balance of my own. The balance I struck was between my admiration for J.A. Kufuor, on the one hand, and my neutrality in the party-politics of Ghana, on the other. I admire Kufuor as a man of achievement and vision. But I am neutral about his political party or its platform. I also judge his policies independently, one issue at a time.

Legend has it that in about 1960 Kwame Nkrumah and Felix Houphouet-Boigny had a wager. The Ivorian leader would respect the market economy and remain close to the West. The Ghanaian President would experiment with a command economy and asserts his independence from Western neo-colonialism. After ten years which country would be better off—Cote d'Ivoire or Ghana?

After ten years the Ivory Coast seemed to have won the wager. Nkrumah had been overthrown in a military coup, civilian politicians had been intimidated or driven into exile, and the Ghanaian economy was a mere shadow of its former prosperity.

More than thirty additional years have passed since then. Under President J.A. Kufuor it is Ghana which has become a model of relative stability and which is emerging slowly as a beacon of prosperity. Cote d'Ivoire is struggling for a new equilibrium between domestic contending forces and a new balance between independent African assertiveness and a continuing special relationship with France.

Perhaps the original wager of 1960 was too simplistic about the comparative causes of stability and prosperity in African countries. The heroic country of yesterday can become the pathetic country of today – and vice-versa. The reasons are much more complex than such issues as which country is neo-colonialist and which one chooses a command economy.

President J.A. Kufuor symbolizes a new dawn in Ghana. He is in reality the first Ghanaian President of this twenty-first century, the first of this new millennium. He brings into the new Ghanaian equation fresh ideas of nation-building and a new energy in the pursuit of development.

Since independence Ghana has alternated between military regimes and civilian ones. It is true that the military regimes have sometimes been exceptionally brutal. Ghana is the only African country, which has through a military regime-executed several former Heads of State.

On the other hand, during the years when Ghana has been under civilian rule, the leaders have been exceptionally well-educated. Kwame Nkrumah still remains the most prolific presidential writer in Africa's postcolonial history. Kofi Busia remains one of the best educated Africans to become Head of State. Dr. Hilla Limann brought new expertise to the highest ranks of governance in Ghana. And now President J.A. Kufuor has brought legal and constitutional sophistication to the highest political office in the land.

Beginning with his degree in Politics, Philosophy and Economics (PPE) from Oxford University and his legal training at an Inn of Court in London, Kufuor has become another intellectual Head of State in Ghana.

Ghana was of course the first Black African country to win independence from colonial rule. Kwame Nkrumah was the first African to become a member of Her Majesty's Privy Council in Britain. William Abraham was the first

African to be elected Fellow of All Soul's College, Oxford. Kofi Annan was the first Black man to become Secretary-General of the United Nations. And now J.A.Kufuor is the first African legal mind to be entrusted with the Rule of Law in an African country this new century.

This book introduces us to this new Ghana of J.A. Kufuor and to his intellectually alert leadership. The book provides some new insights into the experience of Ghana in the era of globalization.

There was a time under Kwame Nkrumah when Ghana tried to be the vanguard of technology. A nuclear research reactor in Ghana enabled Nkrumah to declare proudly: "Socialism without science is void."

There was a time in Ghana when the leadership of Kofi Busia made Ghanaians believe that they had achieved the governance of the philosopher king. A professor was at the helm of the state. And when Adu Boahen made a bid for the presidency, it once again illustrated that some of Ghana's top minds were prepared to compete for political office.

There was a time when Ghana demonstrated that a despot could change and become a genuine democrat. That was the supreme achievement of Jerry Rawlings. His was a remarkable transition from military despotism to a peaceful democratic succession.

In J.A. Kufuor Ghana may at last have arrived in a kingdom of intelligent commonsense. Power has been tamed, economy redirected, and the nation has been given a new sense of purpose. The first President of the new millennium has indeed found a new national mission. We wish him wisdom and fulfillment.

Ali A. Mazrui, **D. Phil (Oxon)**
Director, Institute of Global Cultural Studies,
Albert Schweitzer Professor in the Humanities,
State University of New York at Binghamton.

Introduction

I started my writing career as a political journalist in 1990. The political situation in Ghana was getting better in terms of intellectual discourse. Here was a military Government, of the Provisional National Defense Council, headed by Flt. Lt. J.J. Rawlings that five years back counted for less in the realm of freedom of speech; with sensitive record of brutality to those who dared to talk in dissenting tongues. It was an uncomfortable odyssey in a difficult transition.

But that was at the evening of dying agonies, of what former President Rawlings himself described as the Culture of Silence. The agonies of the early days of the regime could only be imagined.

I worked with mainly the private newspaper media before my semi-retirement in 1998. I was able afterwards, to create some space for independent thinking and reflection. Within the eight years, I wrote and reported on politics for both local and International media and got into contact with many of the leading lights in the political circuit. The main or biggest circulation newspapers in Ghana are still State owed. Working with the noted independent and critical paper—*The Pioneer*, meant some of these players became friends—the former President of Ghana the late Dr. Hilla Limann, Opposition leader and eminent historian Prof. Albert Adu Boahen, President of the Methodist Conference Rev. Dr. Samuel Asante Antwi, Human Rights Activist and lawyer the late Obeng Manu, who tragically passed on in 1998, and the then middle aged lawyer and politician John Agyekum Kufuor.

I collaborated in an earlier book—*Political Reflections on the Motherland* with some of these figures.

These contacts and collaborations were leading posts into the minds of politicians and what they generally do.

This book is about the life of one of these players—J.A. Kufuor who fate decreed would be a president one day. When he did in January 2001, my intension was to keep a distance and from that, observe his navigation into the ways and by-ways of governance. Some months into his presidency, we met by chance at the State House, his official working place before he moved to the seat of Government at the Osu Castle. I requested to write a biography of him not from the official point of view but one in which I would still need his help. He reluctantly agreed. I had also made it known to him that I had already collected some family data two years before, through a family historian—his sister Agnes Addo Kufuor. The two of us have had very irregular but insightful conversations over the years.

I did not foresee that some of the general data of family pedigree would one day be useful for a biography of her brother. The intension at the time was to write an essay on women contribution to economic history in the Gold Coast of nineteenth century using their mother Ama Paa as a case study.

Like many political biographies, this one is offered at a time when our subject is still a president. In order not to pre-empt an assessment of what his first four-year term in office will be like, the work is limited to the time he became an elected president on December 31, 2000.

This way, it becomes easier to reflect or narrate confidently what is already past and do an update in later editions when the present becomes past again.

Secondly, it is being written as a contribution to our political development in which biographies or memoirs of heroes and villains are left unwritten until they develop into an apocrypha; a situation that creates pitfalls for a progressive cutting of the path.

In Chapter One: *A Child May Resemble His Father But Has a Family—The Making of Apagyafie*, I attempt to evaluate an Asante (Akan) belief in matrilineal inheritance and how in a very interesting case J.A. Kufuor fits into the benefits of this. It looks at his growing up and the expectations and dreams that all children nurse.

In *The Journey to Oxford: The Love of Theresa and of Politics*, I try to show how J.A. Kufuor's rich family background, luck as well as perseverance to excel led him to Oxford. His love for Theresa when they met at the Ghana High Commission in London and the consequences of that meeting.

Chapters Three and Four— *Return to Ghana: The Sorcerer's Apprentice* and *Following the Foot-prints of the Fathers*, continue to show how hard work, and luck enabled Kufuor to be embraced by benevolent "political cousins and uncles"— namely Prof. K. A. Busia, Victor Owusu, and William Ofori Atta who were pillars of Ghana's democratic culture after the overthrow of Kwame Nkrumah. They gave him all the opportunities to shine if he so desired.

The Farewell to the Men on Horseback narrates how Kufuor impatiently looked on the advent of military dictatorship in Ghanaian politics and how he thought his years and that of many of his generation were being wasted.

That advent also opened the re-introduction of party politics with the military Government of Rawlings under pressure from Ghanaians and donors— European or Western Governments.

In Chapter Seven, *The Agama Lizard Walks Slowly But it will Get to its Destination*, the story is about how Kufuor by 1998 become a prominent Opposition figure in Ghanaian politics by overcoming a near pariah status within his party. To some, he was not qualified to lead because he lacked the intellectual procedure for that. To others, he was an Asante and by some logic made in the shadows of Victor Owusu, his mentor. Like a badly bruised innocent person mistaken for a terrorist he still emerged a lonely presidential hopeful. He had only destiny, ambition, his gentle giant stature, self-belief and perhaps, the final verdict of the Sorcerer to propel him on. These were the tools for the fulfillment of a childhood dream. Even at this juncture, it was not so clear what fate or decision the gods had made until the long journey ended at sunrise with his unexpected but some say, divine landslide victory. He became the second President of the Fourth Republic of Ghana!!

This book may lack some details in parts and some over-elaboration in others but it is for a purpose. It is written partly to cover the memoirs of Kufuor by a journalist who is also interested in narrative and critical political history. In this, I have tried as much to place the memoirs at the center of these multiple interests. Those who will find the over elaboration may do so especially with the politics of the 1990s in which many of us—Ghanaians and those who kept eyes on events there, were witnesses to but, remember dear reader, that as the days pass, we forget some and as the days roll into years, we leave the next generation sometimes vague remembrances of what we saw.

For the first time in the history of Ghana, we had a Government that served its two terms—eights years in office and was handed over to an old Opposition regime without rancor. It was a success story of smooth transition in Africa adding to few precedents: Leopold Sedar Senghor to Abdou Diouf to Abdoulaye Wade in Senegal, Kenneth Kaunda to Frederick Chiluba in Zambia, Julius Nyerere to Ali Hassan Mwinyi to Benjamin Mkapa in Tanzania and Botswana's long time example of democratic culture.

Like Kwame Nkrumah's leadership of the anti-colonial struggle in the 1960s, the transition brought Ghana a silver lining.

This book will help in part to make us not at least forget all of that. And if it does, the better.

Ivor Agyeman-Duah
Silver Spring, Maryland
September 16, 2002

CHAPTER ONE

A Child May Resemble His Father But Has a Family: The Making of Apagyafie

*The younger generation say: "We no longer rest in the
ancient resting place." Why then do they not throw away
one of the three old hearthstones and leave two?*

—Akan Proverb.

*[Used in warning people against discarding all old tradi-
tions as useless. They are so much a part of man that he
cannot do without them. Three hearthstones are
used to balance the cooking pot.]*

1

A sante New Town (Ash-Town) lies, with its spiraling historical buildings in the northwestern part of Kumasi, the capital of the once powerful Kingdom of Asante.

Many of the storey buildings here were constructed in the 1920s out of Cocoa money. The surrounding villages in Asante grew and still grow Cocoa and at one time contributed in making Ghana the biggest producer of the commodity in the world. The wealth of the people is either out of Cocoa or Gold. The Ashanti Goldfields Company, one of the biggest mines in the world lies some 55km South of Kumasi and people here have family lands and chiefship titles that entitle them to annual Gold remittances.

In the 1920s, many Cocoa and Gold merchants built houses. Asante New Town and Kumasi as a city had also become the center of trade in what was still the Gold Coast (before March 6, 1957, when the Gold Coast became independent of British colonial rule). It was a center to all the ethnic groups in Ghana and immigrants from Sierra Leone, Togo, Burkina Faso, Ivory Coast and a considerable non-African population. In the 1960s, it was estimated that one-sixth of all immigrants that arrived in Ghana settled in Kumasi.

As Jean Allman recounts: Nothing better summarizes the centrality of Cocoa to Asante (or better the Asante perception of Cocoa as the economic backbone of their society) than a local highlife song made popular in the 1950s:

> If you want to send your children to school it is Cocoa,
> If you want to build your house it is Cocoa,
> If you want to marry, it is Cocoa,
> If you want to buy cloth it is Cocoa,
> If you want to buy Lorry, it is Cocoa
> Whatever you want to do in this world,

It is with Cocoa money that you do it.

The huge houses built from Cocoa money impressed residents and visitors to the Asante capital of Kumasi. From Asante New Town through the Feeder Road that led to the neighborhood's main Post Office in the northern sector was situated the palace of the King of Asante, at Manhyia. From the palace in the southwestern direction, only about 200 meters, was the biggest storey building in the whole vicinity—pink in colour and big enough to have 30 rooms with adjoining halls and chambers. It was called Apagyafie. Built in the early 1930s, it was here that John Agyekum Kufuor was born on December 8, 1938 to Nana Ama Dapaah and a local chief—the Kumasi Oyokohene Nana Kwadwo Agyekum.

Nana Ama Dapaah (Ama Paa as she was popularly known) was born in 1903 into an illustrious lineage. Her father was a chief–Nana Kwabena Kufuor of Nkawie who later became Denkyirahene. Kwabena Kufuor's ancestry goes as far as to one of the earlier kings of the 1660s imperial state, Denkyira, called Boa Amponsem. Her mother was Akua Bema Mansa. Bema Mansa's other child—Kwaku Addo Kwarbo was Ama Paa's senior brother. Bema was also the wife of the Asantehene Nana Prempeh I. They had a son called Nana Boakye Prempeh who was born when King Prempeh had been taken to the Seychelles by the British. But the family pedigree goes to the founding of the Asante Empire itself and in a far distant land—three hundred years ago in Denkyira, Western Region of Ghana, where an Asante Royal Osei Tutu (later first king of Asante) married Brimpomaa Sarfowaa and brought her to Kumasi. Sarfowaa is the earliest known ancestor of Ama Paa.

A stock of the Akan people of Ghana and constituting over 55 percent of the population, Asante is a matrilineal society. This means that descent and inheritance of family property is traced through the female or mother's side. An Asante proverb says, "A child may resemble his father but he has a family." Thus, no matter the closeness of a child to the father, the real family is the mother's. This environment at Asante New Town and the belief structure in the matrilineal sense as would be made known, had a great impact on the future president.

Ama Paa grew up without engaging in very serious trading as her contemporaries did. She, however, had seven uncles who were rich and by Akan inheritance tradition, would pass on their wealth to her. These uncles would not only change the destiny of the then young Ama Paa but that of a future Ghana. The uncles were — Nana Kofi Poku (who became Apagyahene), Nana Kwasi Sekyere, Nana Kwabena Mensah or Owusu Afriyie who also became Apagyahene at the age of 10 and took part in the Yaa Asantewaa War of 1900 (the last Asante war against British colonial rule). Nana Poku, Nana Kwaku Jantuah, Nana Yaw Berfi and Kwabena Antwi were the others.

These uncles became Cocoa farmers and sold Cocoa beans to multi-national companies including UAC and SAT.

Yaw Berfi, for instance bought a vast land at Anyinasuso in 1936 and every June, Ama Paa's elder children visited the property to help with the work, came to know the property, and enjoyed the vastness and beauty of their family land.

But it was really Ama Paa's brother Kwarbo, who saw the value of education, and ensured that all of Ama Paa's children would be sent to school. Kwarbo was a great farmer and cultivated Cola Nuts, Coffee and Cocoa at Anyinasuso and Para rubber in Kumasi.

The last of Ama Paa's uncles died in the 1960s. The only woman in the line of inheritance, she automatically inherited a great amount of wealth including houses, farms and cash backed by an interesting family history.

What is now the family house—Apagyafie—was where Ama Paa gave birth to some of her children starting with John Agyekum Kufuor in 1938. The house originally belonged to a Kwahu trader from the Eastern Region of Ghana until Kwabena Mensah purchased it. Prior to this time, Ama Paa had lived at one of her uncle's houses at Kejetia. It was here that she gave birth to her son, Francis Kufuor, who would later become a pioneer Chemistry professor in Ghana and Chairman of the Kwame Nkrumah University of Science and Technology. Agnes Addo Kufuor also known as Nana Akua Durowaa, who later married Asantehene Sir Osei Agyeman Prempeh II was also born at the Kejetia property. Ama Paa's change of residence from Kejetia to Apagyafie at Asante New Town had great impact on the children. Apagyafie was a stones' throw from Manhyia. The original palace of the king, even in the 1920s, was not magnificent and was more like a small forest dwelling. That was why in 1924 when King Prempeh I returned from exile, he first settled at Asafo until the Colonial Government built him a new palace. This notwithstanding, residency close to the royal residence at Manhyia had significance to those who owned property in Kumasi and the Apagyafie was no exception.

The greatest blessing upon the Kufuor children, however, came from their mother, Ama Paa. As Kwame Anthony Appiah tells us in *In My Father's House: Africa in the Philosophy of Culture*, "Never assume that individual women cannot gain power under patriarchy." After having her children, Ama Paa protected the inherited family wealth against usurpers and strong men in a way that has become a marvel—fighting court battles and winning them. She also invested and added to the Apagyafie with money earned from farming and trading in Cocoa. By 1950, all her nine children—Francis Addo Kufuor, Agnes Addo Kufuor, John Agyekum Kufuor, Kwame Addo

Kufuor (who later converted the Kejetia property into the Kufuor Clinic in Kumasi), George Addo Kufuor, Mariam Addo Kufuor, Cecilia Akoto Campbell, Rebecca Duodu and Josephine (Kankam) Annin—had moved to Apagyafie to live with her and their uncles.

Ama Paa's children were not all from one marriage. Agnes Addo Kufuor's father—Kwadwo Gyei—was an influential goldsmith in Takyimantia, formerly part of Asante but now in the Brong Ahafo Region. She was living with the father when her uncle sent for her to attend school in Kumasi. At Apagyafie, all the children were raised under a common code of tradition and hard work. As it was the case in the 1920s, the girls took after their mother's trade.

Ama Paa was a first class designer of beads and so all of them especially Agnes Kufuor learned the trade. She also took them through cookery lessons. Since every woman, it was believed, would one day leave her parents for a husband, cooking was a mandatory art for it could sustain or sometimes break a marriage.

There were no pipe facilities at that time and so all the girls would fetch water from a near-by well for domestic use.

The five boys cleaned the shoes of their uncles, pounded the evening Fufu—Asante's favorite delicacy for a dinner for over 30 people who lived in the house and also strangers.

Though as a boy he never lived under the tutelage of his father, J.A. Kufuor was already developing interest in Asante's cultural values. He would accompany his father to the Manhyia Palace where the Asantehene would sit in court on Mondays and Thursdays to adjudicate cases—civic and land litigation. The young J.A. Kufuor, less then 10 years, would insist to wear cloth like his father to the Palace and listened pretentiously to proceedings. He and his brothers did not only take part in the court's processions during the Adae Festival or other such activities, but danced to Fontomfrom, Kete and Adowa renditions.

The Oyoko Stool and clan which Kufuor's father was the head is a very important stool created as part of the political structure of Asante in the early 1700s. The clan is one to which the Asante royalty with the Asantehene as the primus interparas belongs. Every Asantehene literally has an Oyokohene as uncle.

In the olden days, it was the Oyokohene who had the power to declare war. Then and now, an Oyokohene is supposed to be intelligent and also be the king's advisor.

The status of being a warrior and the king's advisor was such that the British colonial authorities exiled in 1896 the 'troublesome' Oyokohene Kwadwo Agyekum together with King Prempeh I to Cape Coast in the Central Region (of what is today Ghana) and eventually, to the Seychelles Island. Agyekum died in the Seychelles. His successor, Kwame Nkansah was also exiled to Accra, the future capital of Ghana by the British in the early 1900s where he also died.

Before these warriors and advisors, there was the second Oyokohene, Kwapong Diawuo (successor to the first Oyokohene who later became Juabenhene, Adarkwa Yiadom) who served as advisor to King Osei Tutu. It was this warrior that Kwadwo Agyekum named his son John Agyekum Kufuor alias Kofi Diawuo, after.

Typical of children born in the 1930s and well into the post-colonial era, Kufuor has two names. Kofi Diawno is derived from the fact of being born on a Friday(Kofi among the Akan) and in memory of his gallant ancestor Diawuo.

As a christian, he had to be given a baptismal or christian name so he had John and the father's name, Agyekum. In keeping with his mother's unusual Asante tradition, Kufuor, was added to it. It is interesting how this practice which was uncommon in the Asante of 1940s now has assumed national and even international dimensions. Now, a married or wedded woman would maintain her father's name and add that of her husband's as a last name. This has become part of family identity and in some sense an independent womanhood affair that could in a traditional or modern way challenge marriage definition and perhaps the extent of a man's control over his wife.

Notwithstanding a history of his immediate ancestors against colonial rule, Kufuor's father lived as a boy with a British family in Kumasi in the 1900s. Without any formal education, that association exposed him to many good tidings.

According to Kufuor's matrilineal family source, Kwadwo Agyekum was so curious after Kufuor's birth that like Saul of old in the famous mid-night visit to the medium at Endor, he traveled all the way to Sampa(near what is today the Ivory Coast) to find out from an acknowledged sorcerer the fate of his child.Because the Kufuor story has a happy ending, we may say the sorcerer really knew his job.

Apart from being a cherished advisor when he became the Oyokohene to Asantehene Osei Kyeretwie, or Prempeh II, Kwadwo Agyekum was instrumental in the restoration of the Asante Confederacy Council in 1935.

After the last Asante war against the British in 1900, a war popularly called the Yaa Asantewaa War, in memory of the Queen of Ejisu-Asante who led it, the feeling was that the 200 year old empire had ended with the defeat of the Asantes.

King Prempeh and all his gallant chiefs had been taken into exile in the Seychelles. When Prempeh I returned in 1924, the empire was short of pockets of smaller independent states. It was during his time that all the states decided to unite again as a kingdom.

Again our guiding proverb: A child may resemble his

father but has a family. But in the case of Kufuor, both ways, his matrilineal family history and his patrilineal, lead to virtually the same direction or roots, King Osei Tutu who died in 1717. The direction or roots is partly bloodline and partly politics, empire building.

Could it also be that this investigation into his pedigree leads us to another Asante proverb: The matri-clan is like the forest. If you stand afar, it looks the same but when you get closer, you find that each tree has its own branches.

Ama Paa had grown convinced in the early 1950s that her teenage son (tall-looking for his age) would one day become Apagyahene. The Apagya Stool was created by Asantehene Osei Tutu Kwame Asibe Bonsu (1804-1823) for his son, Owusu Gyamaduaa. It was a hereditary stool for sons of Asantehenes from the house to which the Kufuors' belonged.

What however deepened J.A. Kufuor's interest and respect for traditional values was the marriage of his sister Agnes to the Asantehene, Prempeh II in the early 1940s. Thus, his father was not only an important chief at the palace but he had become a brother-in-law of the King. He learned the palace language and its associated proverbs as well as the formation of Asante as an empire and how it progressed since the early 1700s. Agnes Addo Kufuor recalls:

> J.A. Kufuor was very reflective, quiet and always deep in his thoughts. Kwame Addo Kufuor was the noisy one—the one who would always entertain us with jokes. We thought he would be a Lawyer.

In the same 1950s, Christianity was challenging certain traditional or cultural values in Asante. Asante's contact with Christianity dated back to the 1840s when the Asantehene Kwaku Duah I who reigned from 1838-1867 accepted the Wesleyan missionary, Thomas Birch Freeman to Asante in 1841. Later in the 1870s there was Father Moore, a Catholic missionary who also came to Kumasi and later established the Catholic Church. The Presbyterians led by the head missionary from Switzerland Ramsyer also came and clashed with the Asantehene Kofi Karkari in the early 1870s over what they perceived to be barbaric practices by the chiefs and which needed replacement with Christian values.

It was however the conversion in the early 1900s by Asantehene Prempeh II to Christianity in the Seychelles Islands that turned many Asante chiefs to Christianity. Prempeh became an Anglican in the Seychelles and on his return the Asante Royalty became forever Anglican. Thus Apaga, J.A. Kufuor's family house became Anglican, and so did his father's. Other chiefs joined the Catholics and the Presbyterians.

J.A. Kufuor went to the St. Cyprian Anglican Church as regularly as he went to the palace. He even became a singer and enjoyed the hymns as much as he enjoyed the praise singing poetry that accompanied the Asantehene's procession and often in memory of gallant Asante soldiers.

To many people J.A. Kufuor could be contradictory, strong believer in traditional values and a staunch Anglican. But that has to do with his background and strong principles. The same conviction that led him – in 1972 to join the Catholic Church. After the overthrow of the Second Republic of Ghana through the military take-over, he was arrested as Deputy Minister of Foreign Affairs and imprisoned. Throughout his stay in prison neither the Anglican Bishop of Accra nor any of the leading church elders visited him. Other political prisoners had their bishops come and pray for them. Bishop Peter Akwasi Sarpong, the Catholic Bishop of Kumasi traveled to visit and pray for him. After his release, his sister Agnes advised him to take God seriously and so he did by joining the Catholic Church in anger and also to be sure that when he needed God, at least his representative would be there to inspire him.

Schooling started early for J.A. Kufuor in the mid 1940s at the Asem Government Boys School in Kumasi. One of the very few schools at the time, many leaders passed through here. His brilliance or otherwise was not very clear. This was because term reports were not given making it difficult to assess a ward's progress in School. The young Kufuor also found happiness in other things, played football at what was called Cricket Pitch, which is now the Manhyia Park.

With some basic education at Government Boys, J.A.'s uncle—Kwarbo, decided to send him and his brothers to Osei Tutu Boarding School about 7 miles from Kumasi. The Boarding school had emerged as the best in town and their uncle ever dreaming of the best sent them there. Here term reports were given and so the brilliance of Kufuor was emerging—topping his class in many areas and showing discipline in the conduct of his academic pursuits. It was from here that his elder brother Francis Kufuor and two of his sisters would pass to Achimota School in Accra. Kwame Addo Kufuor would also go to Achimota.

1954 was a dangerous year in the political transition in Ghana. Kwame Nkrumah, who had returned from the United Kingdom to become Secretary-General of the United Gold Coast Convention, UGCC, an anti-colonial political organization founded in Saltpond in 1947, was a political agitator impatient to see the end of British rule. He had had strong disagreements with the founders of the UGCC—Dr. J. B. Danquah, Edward Akuffo Addo, Obetsebi-Lamptey, William Ofori Atta, Ako Adjei and resigned to form the Convention Peoples' Party (CPP). By this time, Kwame Nkrumah who was on the verge of leading Ghana to independence, became the obvious leader and advocate of African nationalism and Pan African unity in the post-World War II era.

People in the Kingdom of Asante however resented their about to be real assimilation into a nation-state.

As Jean Allman says, "The National Liberation Movement demanded Asante self-determination in the face of Kwame Nkrumah's blueprint for a unitary government in an independent Ghana. It did not only pose a serious threat to the stability of "Nkrumah's government in the last years before independence," but shattered the illusion, present since 1951, that the Gold Coast's transition to full self-rule would proceed with rapidity and order."

The leader of this Asante Movement that opposed Nkrumah's unitary concept was Baffour Osei Akoto, Senior Linguist of the Asantehene Sir Osei Agyeman Prempeh II. Akoto is the father of one of Ama Paa's children. Ama Paa had supported the Movement's agitation for federal government and the preservation of Asante cultural values. Meetings were held in her Apaga house and she gave large sums of money for political organization and strategies. The first country car, Jeep, to be used for political campaign by the NLM later United Party was donated by Apagyafie.

It was such visitation to the house by Baffour Osei Akoto and other first generation nationalist leaders such as J.B. Danquah, William Ofori Atta, Joe Appiah, John Tsiboe, Victor Owusu, Prof. Kofi Abrefa Busia (Prime Minister of the Second Republic) that ignited J.A. Kufuor's interest in politics. These people were heroes to Nkrumah's Opposition. They had been trained at Oxford, Cambridge and the University of London. The beauty of their training, how they carried themselves, served as the first political inspiration for the young Kufuor and his brother Kwame Addo Kufuor. Busia and Victor Owusu became the mentors of John Agyekum and to a lesser extent of Kwame Addo Kufuor.

Apart from normal visiting, Busia, a very religious man (Methodist by denomination) would come to the house to pray before party rallies and especially at a time when his life was endangered because of his opposition to Kwame Nkrumah.

But Nkrumah also visited Ama Paa's house. Jean Allman asked her on August 6, 1984, — "What did you dislike about Nkrumah?" and Ama Paa replied:

I liked nothing at all. He never really did anything wrong. He even stayed in this very house when he was a child. But I didn't side with him on his idea of Freedom, Freedom.

Political intolerance was very high and political affiliation was more a family heritage. Kwame Addo Kufuor told me that as a teenager, he and many people found Danquah and others difficult to understand though they admired them. "They were too serious for the period in which they found themselves." On the contrary, he and his brothers enjoyed the picnic, the brass band music that were characteristic of the CPP rallies. They got electrified "with the insincere talk and messages of people like Krobo Adusei and Atta Mensah." It did not surprise them that people paid money to attend CPP rallies. Addo Kufuor recounts:

One day I went out to buy toffee across the street under our house maid—Afua's guidance. We ended up attending a CPP rally. I had never seen someone talking through a loudspeaker and so I got fascinated and got closer to Bentill Casely-Hayford who was talking. In response to a question on the spur of the moment, I said Nkrumah was a hero because the white people (British Colonialists) were cheating us. The crowd got electrified but Afua immediately left me to complain that I had publicly become CPP. I was severely punished.

The family discipline at home was stiffer than at school. "Our teachers did not need to correct us because we had been disciplined before we went to school," commented Addo Kufuor. In fact, the preparation at home included training the children to develop a high sense of discipline and responsibility, but given their youthful age, they were not able always to control their political excitements. Addo Kufuor was only eleven years of age and certainly was carried by youthful exuberance when he attended the CPP political rally in Kumasi. He still remembers Nkrumah's car number—AS 38—and his experience tells of the political temperature at the time.

As J.A. Kufuor says, he was also to witness the other side of politics, the violence associated with political campaigns. The Apagyafie is situated between what was the CPP regional office in Kumasi and the NLM office. The NLM claimed over ninety percent of Asante's support. In the heat of political rivalries and campaigning, Twumasi-Ankrah, Propaganda Secretary of the CPP murdered the Secretary of the NLM Emmanuel Yaw Baffoe on October 9, 1954. This was interpreted as a political murder. As Allman recalls, "it unleashed the frustrations of many; it was a powerful catalyst for mass mobilization and action. As a result of the nearly ungovernable state of Kumasi and its surrounding villages, the government announced less than forty-eight hours after Baffoe's murder that it had suspended the issuing of permits for any processions or public meetings."

It was in 1954 that J.A. Kufuor passed his Common Entrance Examination to go to secondary school. He very much wanted to go to Achimota School like his brother

Francis and two of his sisters Mrs. Campbell and Mrs. Duodu. In those days, one had to pass an interview before formal admission to a school. The Headmaster of Achimota traveled to Kumasi (to Prempeh College) to interview all who had selected Achimota. Surprising himself Kufuor did not pass the interview. "I was not tidy in my dressing and I am sure that I did not make the necessary impression."

His uncle who was also the Apagyahene at the time would not hear of this and so arranged to send him to Britain for secondary education.

In the process of getting ready to travel, the Apagyahene's cousin, Mr. Mensah Bonsu, a businessman in Kumasi visited and persuaded the family to send Kufuor to Prempeh College which to him was as good as Achimota. He was sure Prempeh would admit the young man. Truly they did and so J.A. Kufuor missed his chance of secondary education in Britain. Because he was admitted late he missed the earlier weeks of class.

He was put in one of the dormitories, Butler House. Because the school was not far from home and he also knew many of the students there, he enjoyed life at the school. The school itself was new, less than ten years old and built by the Scottish Presbyterian missionaries in memory of the Asantehene Prempeh II. Some of his mates, including his best friend were Dr. Kwame Appiah Poku, I. K. Apea whom he started school with at Government Boys School, his cousin Kwame Agyei Kufuor and Nana Osei Bonsu, currently the Asante Mamponghene. At Prempeh Kufuor enjoyed sports. It soon got round that the young man from Apagyafie was not only topping his class in many of the subjects but that he was a good football player, played cricket as well as table tennis. In athletics, he represented the school in the annual inter-colleges and was the school's champion.

J.A. Kufuor, if he had any leadership skills, did not exhibit at this point because students' politics and leadership was reserved for those in Sixth Form but whatever there was at that level, a dormitory monitor, he became.

Excelling in his studies, Kufuor took more to the Arts and developed interest in History, Latin, Geography, English and other related Arts subjects. Students were also mandated to study any of the natural sciences and Kufuor opted for Biology in which he obtained an A at the final level.

By the time he got to the fifth year, Kufuor was already a superstar intellectually and was as popular in sports as in academics. At the close of school in 1959, he collected five of the six prizes annually presented to best students. The sixth prize, Geography, was given to another student who received the same points, at the plead of the subject instructor.

At the prize ceremony that year, Kufuor's brother-in-law the Asantehene, Osei Agyeman Prempeh II, sat at the dais with Kufuor's sister Agnes.

After collecting the third prize, the Headmaster, an Englishman from Cambridge, called Mr. Arthur Lewis, nicknamed him "A Kufuor" alluding to his 'A' status as he collected the remaining prizes. After the ceremony when the Asantehene and the other dignitaries had retired for refreshment, Kufuor was called over and it was there that to the amazement of the Headmaster, the Asantehene introduced him as his-brother-in-law. Mr. Lewis in a testimony for Kufuor after he had completed his studies in December 1958, wrote, "Constantly good. He has occupied one of the first three places in his class for the last three years. Usually tops. We expected him to return to the sixth form as he passed the entrance examination."

Interestingly, Kufuor was not to go to Sixth Form at Prempeh College or any other school in the country. He had done exceedingly well at the entrance examination that will enable him go to Sixth Form. He had emerged among the best ten students throughout the country and was also the eighth 'Best Arts Student' in the country with an aggregate of nine. No school would refuse him admission. Such was the results that he could go to a university or Law School in England without passing through the 'A' level education.

The young man from Apagyafie had started life on a very promising intellectual note and looked to the future with great determination.

CHAPTER TWO

The Journey to Oxford:
The Love of Theresa and Politics

You will ever remember that all the end of study is to make you a good man and a useful citizen.

—John Adams

Having short-circuited his education with such brilliance, J.A. Kufuor, the ordinary Akan youth in search of a vision and a future arrived in London in April 1959 at the age of 20. Full of ambition, his target was to read Law. Many youth of his generation could hardly be entrusted by fate or luck with the kind of wealth and investment that had been made available to him.

Many African students who were studying in London at the time were on British Council or Commonwealth scholarships, two of the educational incentives given to students in the about to be independent colonies of Britain. Even with these, they had to work part-time to supplement their stipends and support their families.

J.A. Kufuor arrived in London without these difficulties, not even the sometimes inconvenient week-end shopping. His family had paid his fees. The mother had bought a house in Northwest of London near Muswell Hill, a prime area and the favorite of many a Jew. Two of his sisters —Mariam Kufuor and Cecilia Akoto Campbell were already living here. And so he went to a family embrace.

One of his biggest influences once in London was U.V. Campbell, a Jamaican who was married to his sister Cecilia. A well-known legal brain among many Afro-Caribbean students and the British establishment at the time, Mr. Campbell topped the Bar examination in his year and was one of the few to be awarded a first class.

Day by day conversation deepened Kufuor's affection for his brother-in-law. In May 1959, Kufuor was very sure he wanted to study law and so Mr. Campbell took him to the Inns of Court to register as a law student at Lincoln's Inn. There, they met a friend of Campbell who after examining Kufuor's school certificate from Ghana got so impressed with his distinguished record including his skipping of Sixth Form education. Kufuor was assured he did not need any more qualification to enroll at Lincoln's

Inn in the class of May/June 1959.

By 1961, when he was 22 years, Kufuor had completed the first part of the Bar examination. The courses were reasonably smooth and he did not have any failures in the seven subjects that constituted the part one of the Bar. But this did not come easy. It meant that six of the seven days, he had to lock himself and be buried in his books.

Immediately after the first part of the Bar, he set himself preparing for his Bar finals which comprised thirteen subjects.

Kufuor traveled to London in 1959, the same year as Professor K.A. Busia left Holland to take residence in England. The Professor knew the Kufuor family from the various visits to Apagyafie in Kumasi. It was therefore not surprising when Professor Busia visited the Kufuor children in London when he arrived in the city in 1959. The last time J.A. Kufuor had seen him was in 1955 when the Professor visited Ama Paa at Apagyafie. That was two years before Ghana's independence. By June 1959,   however, Professor Busia had been forced to flee his opposition parliamentary post in the new Ghana into exile in Holland by the political actions of the Nkrumah regime. News of the Professor's impending visit was therefore an exciting one and it was delivered on one December day in 1959 by Adwoa Agyeman, a house mate at the Kufuor residence in London, when she returned from town. Adwoa was the daughter of the eminent Mr. I. K. Agyeman of Kumasi and one time patron of K.A. Busia. In fact, Busia in his youthful days lived at the old man's residence in Kumasi.

In a long conversation during the announced visit, Professor Busia wished to find out what Kufuor was doing, and when he told the Professor that he was preparing for the Bar examination, Busia continued his inquiry and asked of what the young man wanted to do after the examination. Without hesitation, Kufuor said he wanted to go to Oxford. When the Professor asked which college at Oxford, he could not tell since he did not know the colleges but all he wanted to do as he told the Professor was "I want to go to Oxford University."

Prof. Busia explained the Oxford system to Kufuor since he had himself attended University College of Oxford and studied Constitutional Law under a leading Oxford scholar Prof. K. C. Wheare. By 1959, Prof. Wheare had become the Rector of Exeter College. K.A. Busia promised that when Kufuor decided which College he wanted to attend, he would be one of his referees. Kufuor decided there and then and told Busia that, "If your tutor is still alive and teaching at Oxford then he would be the one I will want to study under." The Professor promised to put in a word for him.

Busia as an academic celebrity was well-known in the Gold Coast and Ghana. His Oxford education and his exceptional performance at that venerated university made him the darling of many upcoming students. With some exaggeration, which was really not far from the esteem he enjoyed, but which could also be a coincidence, his name Busia was defined as the 'Best University Student in Africa.' Many young men believed this and used him as a model but as time passed and as many realized that he was not the only person in his family with that name, the coincidence became more romantic. How many 'Best University Student in Africa' did this particular family have? This was because some other people bore the name but were still illiterates in his hometown of Wenchi in the Brong Ahafo region.

For Kufuor, however, the meeting with Professor Busia was very important. Strengthened with the possibility of admission Kufuor put in his application to Oxford in 1960. The next year, a letter came from Oxford inviting him to a meeting with the Rector of Exeter College and so he traveled from London to Oxford and found Prof. K.C. Wheare, who was quite old, in his office. Prof. Wheare told Kufuor at the meeting, "We received your application. We understand you are reading for the Bar." (Normally one would read the degree before reading the professional Bar but he had to do it differently because of circumstances).

Kufuor with all humility had responded, "That is true professor."

"There is a gentleman here that you should meet called Mr. D. D. Hall who is a Law tutor. He will asses and find out if you are up to the standard." Prof. Wheare told Kufuor. Whilst waiting patiently, Mr. Hall came to the Rector's Lodge for the meeting and after a long conversation asked Kufuor, "Are you sure you can pass the Bar final in the short time you have set for yourself?" With some confidence almost boarding on a cheek, Kufuor had replied, "Of course I will pass." But the conversation did not end there. Mr. Hall virtually gave the caveat, "If you pass you have been admitted. But you better pass otherwise you cannot come."

After the drill with Mr. Hall, Prof. Wheare intimated that a nice recommendation letter had been received from Prof. Busia. Kufuor was excited after the meeting and thanked them for the showers of traveling mercies from them. He left for London after that encounter with only one thing standing between his admission to Oxford, to pass the Bar examination.

The results of the Bar examination, as it was the tradition those days, was published in *The Times* of London that May. Kufuor had passed, and the joy with which the news was received was immeasurable, his confidence was boosted. Surprisingly, by the time Kufuor finished his Bar examination in April and prior to the release of the results in May, a letter came from Oxford offering him a place at

Exeter College. Subsequent communication from Oxford was the long list of books that were to be read before getting into residence in September of 1961. Kufuor also communicated the good news of developments in England to his uncle and mother in Ghana.

Exeter College, which the young Kufuor found himself, is one of the thirty official colleges of the University of Oxford and the six permanent private halls. Established in 1314, it is one of the oldest learning institutions in the world.

Since the twentieth century, the College has expanded with new buildings. The founder of the school, Walter de Stapeldon, became Bishop of Exeter and Treasurer of England under King Edward II. The College was originally established as an all male institution.

By the time Kufuor arrived, the College had already become a Liberal Arts one. But the College still had a conservative outlook with women being admitted as undergraduates for the first time in 1978.

Kufuor enrolled in Law for the first two terms and did what at the time was called Law Moderation. One had to pass this programme to continue studies at Oxford. With that hurdle cleared, Kufuor decided to go to Ghana to be called to the Ghana Bar in March of 1962. He had already been called to the British Bar but his intension was to practice in Ghana in future.

The Ghana he wanted to return to was however becoming a disappointment in his eyes. After the Kwame Nkrumah Government passed the notorious Preventive Detention Act, a precursor of the One-party state in 1958, people were literally living in fear. The justification had been the several assassination attempts on Kwame Nkrumah's life, which he blamed on the Opposition.

Nkrumah's Preventive Detention Act had a blatant goal of locking up many of the Opposition members.

Leading figures such as Baffour Osei Akoto, Kufuor's stepfather, Messrs R.R. Amponsah and M.K. Apaloo had already been detained.

Busia himself had very early in his opposition to Nkrumah escaped detention and was smuggled through the Ivory Coast to Europe where he engaged in university teaching.

In 1961, after the detention of Dr. J. B. Danquah, Mr. Victor Owusu and over forty others, Prof. Busia decided to leave his professorial chairs at The Hague and Leiden in Holland, to enable him oppose Nkrumah effectively from England.

Kufuor was saddened by these events and was only cheered up by his re-union with his mother and the memories that Apagyafie had for his life. He returned to Oxford after the Bar calling in Ghana. He realized after returning to Oxford that his interest in Law was waning but developed an interest in Politics, Philosophy and Economics (PPE) a very popular programme believed to enlighten people with the desire to go into serious politics. Once in Oxford, he went to see the Rector and told him about his new interest. The Rector and his Law tutors were amazed because of his standing performance but after some persistence, he was allowed to do the PPE in a record of two years and thus obtained the degree in1964.

The weather in London was British all right-all four seasons were unpredictable. Life at Oxford was, however, enjoyed to the brim. The dominant spirit and its sensibilities swept over its students, and Kufuor had the good fortune to come face to face with the most brilliant students from all over the world and also the craziest. Kufuor enjoyed the Oxford Union since it afforded him the opportunity to meet the greats of Great Britain. In those days, it was difficult to see people like Harold Macmillan or Harold Wilson, Enoch Powell and others. Many of these people who were themselves Oxonians would come to attend the Union's meetings and sometimes give lectures. It was at the Union that he met Tom Mboya; the Kenyan political activist who was campaigning in radical measure for the end of British colonial rule in Kenya. He had come to talk to Rhodes scholars at Rhodes House.

There were few Ghanaians at that time in Oxford but they were smart people who would influence generations to come. Prof. William Abraham was an All Souls Fellow at The College of All Souls of The Faithful which meant sheer intellectual power at Oxford; there were also Kwesi Wiredu who would later become a great Philosopher, and his brother Kissi; Kwame Arhin later to become Director of the Institute of African Studies at the University of Ghana, Dr. Charles Van Dyke, late Kwamena Phyllis and few others. In 1962, Nana Akuffo Addo, son of a prominent Ghanaian lawyer Edward Akuffo Addo, also went to Oxford.

All these encounters, which Kufuor cherished in London and also at Oxford, none would be as lasting as the one with Theresa, a young Ghanaian lady he met in London on July 1, 1961 at the Ghana High Commission. It was an anniversary celebration of Ghana's attainment of Republican status. Kufuor had completed Law studies and this lady who had also studied Nursing in Edinburgh for four years was going to the Oxford University Hospital to continue a Mid-wifery course. The coincidence tickled Kufuor but it also marked the beginning of their friendship. In conversation it became clear that Theresa Mensah or Nee Mensah had lived in Kumasi previously and that her brother was the well-known economist J.H. Mensah.

From the first invitation to go out and the others that followed, Kufuor and Theresa settled in fine in Oxford as students. Theresa was friendly and supportive. Occasionally she would prepare him Ghanaian food as they strengthened their friendship. He later said:

I realized I was in love with Theresa and so when I decided to do the right thing—to get married, I was convinced she was the right choice.

Quite quickly and to the amazement of many of the few friends he had, Kufuor decided to marry Theresa within two years of knowing her and when he was two years from finally leaving Oxford. The engagement was fixed for July 1962 at his mother's home near Muswell Hill and Barima Kwaku Adusei, an Asante royal who later became the King of Asante, Otumfuo Opoku Ware II was invited by Kufuor to preside over the ceremony. Two months after, there was the real wedding at Bloomington Catholic Church opposite The Harrods. After the wedding, the couple returned to Oxford again for Kufuor to complete studies. But because they would not be staying longer in Oxford, they rented a flat at the fashionable Woodstock Avenue, near St. Anthony's College.

On September 6, 1963, just a year after the wedding, Theresa gave birth to a son, John Addo Kwarbo Kufuor whom Kufuor named for his beloved uncle.

Kufuor explained why things were getting so fast for him:

I was too serious. I also wanted a focus. I just did not want to be distracted at all. I wanted to do things quickly and go back home and be involved in politics, to try and shape things.

Though Kufuor might have been a serious and focused young man, it was not without some other love stories. Soliciting for personal information especially love stories of people who have assumed eminent status for biographies is hard to get. Those who know may not want to offend and biographical subjects do not give you lead

27

contacts on these.

When I asked Kufuor to talk to me about his ex-girl-friends, he asked in return, "How can you be sure I had some?"

Later some of these speculations about the ex-girl-friends would be questioned in a newspaper — *The Ghanaian Chronicle* assessment of the NPP's run-up to the Congress in 1992.

Immediately after successfully completing his course, father and mother left Oxford with the baby John, for London where Kufuor then 25, had secured employment with the Ghana Commercial Bank Branch.

He was made Manager and Legal Officer at the Bank. After working for three months, Kufuor unexpectedly had to leave for Ghana with the family. Having completed his studies, his mother did not understand why he should live in London. She had not only missed her children who were all studying abroad but she was getting worried about the management of the family property. Francis Kufuor was outside the country   studying so were two other sisters and Kufuor being the next of kin was needed at home by the mother.

The late Maxwell Owusu who had traveled from Ghana to London had firm instructions from Nana Ama Paa to J.A. Kufuor to return. He also had two first class tickets from Nana Ama Paa for his son and daughter-in-law. So Kufuor left London in late December of 1964 in the middle of a severe winter. But the family had increased again. Kufuor had his first daughter–Nana Ama Kufuor on November 29, 1964, whom he had named for his mother. The baby was some few weeks old when the mother wrapped her in winter clothes with John in the care of his father. They boarded the MV Owero that arrived in Tema in January of 1965.

He had been abroad for six years. The first part of J.A.

Kufuor's journey as an Akan boy in search of education and a better future had ended on a promising note and even beyond – he was a father of two children.

The second part of testing the waters on a national stage was just staring in his face.

CHAPTER THREE

Retturn to Ghana: The Sorcerer's Apprentice

I cannot at this stage expect the nation to offer me any thanks for my 34 years of single-hearted devotion to the cause, to have been able to give Ghana not only the clarion call of liberation when "the hour struck" but also to have discovered the glory of our ancient GHANA name and of our philosophy of God, "Nyankopon" as the supreme ancestor and the ideal head of every Ghanaian family. But although I do not expect any kind of thanks now for giving our country's several tribes the basic foundation of a common nationhood-GHANA- of which the people first became fully aware during the 100th celebration of the Bond of 1844, I entertain the hope that my country men and women too will leave me alone to enjoy quietly my poverty in my ripe age of six and sixty years and not seek to pile greed on to the glory of my graying hairs.

—Joseph Boakye Danquah

In 1964, the year Kufuor returned to Ghana, was not the best of times. Kwame Nkrumah had declared Ghana a one-party State by parliamentary approval since the CPP dominated Parliament. J.B. Danquah and the other liberal democrats who had invited Kwame Nkrumah from London to become the Secretary-General of the newly formed anti-colonial movement, the United Gold Coast Convention in 1947, were in prison. Danquah was to die in prison from a heart attack in February 1965, some few months from the time he wrote a protest letter (which is   extracted as an epigraph for this chapter), to the Speaker and Members of Parliament. There was a complete culture of silence since more often, dissent was tantamount to subversion of the Government.

The economic and social conditions were not getting better. Ghana as a declared socialist country in the era of the Cold War, was not getting much development and financial assistance or direct foreign investment from the industrialized countries. Pan Africanism had become not only the Foreign Policy at the time of its greatest and visionary advocate, Kwame Nkrumah, but it was also affecting the domestic management of the Ghanaian economy.

Life was dismal and shops were empty and the people were spiritually depressed.

The second generation of well-trained Ghanaian lawyers and politicians were ready to take the mantle from the first. Among them was Victor Owusu, descendant of the great fetish priest Okomfo Anokye, the principal advisor of the founding of the Asante Empire in the 1700s: Victor Owusu had been trained at the Universities of London and Nottingham through an Asanteman Scholarship scheme and on his return, had established a practice called Komfo Anokye Chambers.

J.A. Kufuor joined Komfo Anokye Chambers. The

Chambers was also a political circuit because Victor Owusu was an acknowledged Opposition heavyweight to Kwame Nkrumah and in terms of legal practice, he was also one of the best in the country. Kufuor joined as a junior partner. Other lawyers in the practice were Messrs Owusu Yaw and John Owusu Afriyie.

Kufuor had barely found his feet when a little over a year after Nana Ama's arrival, he became a father to his second daughter—Yaa Sah Kufuor on November 4, 1965. So far, the average age interval had been a little over a year for his three children. Two more, Edward Agyekum Kufuor born on February 16, 1968, and Kofi Owusu Afriyie Mensah born on June 16, 1972, closed the making of his family.

At 34 when some of his colleagues were about to get married and have children, Kufuor had closed that chapter of his life with three boys and two girls.

Four years into practice, Ghana experienced its first military intervention in politics, the overthrow of Kwame Nkrumah and his Convention Peoples' Party on February 24, 1966. Nkrumah was travelling to Hanoi, Vietnam, to mediate in the Asian crisis at the time. His Pan-African agenda had entered an Asian territory to create Afro-Asian ties.

The coup, which was well greeted, had elements of the Central Intelligence Agency machination mingling with internal Ghanaian resentment of the trend of political direction of the country. Nkrumah had become anti-American, a darling of the East, or the Socialist bloc. Nkrumah damned the United States with an epistle in his *Neo-colonialism: The Last Stages of Imperialism*, a book fraught with the like-thinking of the first practitioner, perhaps of modern socialist ideology, Lenin.

Soon after the coup, Victor Owusu was invited by the coup leaders of the military and police that constituted the National Liberation Council (NLC), to become the Attorney-General of Ghana. So Owusu Yaw became the senior person at the Chambers and J.A. Kufuor, the next in command.

All this while, Kufuor, who was convinced he wanted to become a professional politician had become the growing apprentice to Victor and was only waiting for the first opportunity to knock on the door. He had to however continue his law practice till 1967 when that opportunity came.

Mr. Mensah Bonsu who was the Town Clerk of Kumasi, had retired from the service. Kufuor saw that as the time to enter into public office. Assuming that position would, he presumed, immediately give him the public profile he wanted. He was by this time 28 years and many in Kumasi considered him too young but he also wanted to prove that he was a responsible young man.

The Public Service Commission invited about six people including him for an interview and he was eventually selected. He worked the job for three years, from 1967 to 1969.

The three years exposed him to high public policy formulation and management. Given his legal experience, he had hoped that he would be invited to the Constitutional Assembly that wrote the Second Republican Constitution in 1969 but that was not to be. He, however, retired as Town Clerk when he was elected as the Member of Parliament for Atwima Nwabagya in the Asante Region.

He had to move to Atwima Nwabagya in what was at the time, a little village, because he had not built enough clout to challenge Dr. Alex Atta Yaw Kyerematen. A great cultural avant-garde, the late Kyerematen had also been Town Clerk before Mr. Mensah Bonsu but he had resigned to establish the Ghana National Cultural Centre. Well-known all over Kumasi, he was one of the early peo-

ple to obtain degrees from Oxford and Cambridge. After
the overthrow of Kwame Nkrumah, the National Liberation Council invited Dr. Kyerematen to be the Minister of
Local Government. With the advent of the Constituent
Assembly, Kufuor had been told that Kyerematen was
interested in representing Kumasi and so he had to go to
Atwima.

> After assessing the situation, I found out that I could
> not just put myself against this titan as Kumasi peo-
> ple saw him even though I was ambitious.

At Atwima Nwabagya, the chiefs and the district
assembly members blessed the son of the soil, still in his
graceful youth.

CHAPTER FOUR

Following the Footprints of the Fathers

All men dream: but not equally. Those who dream by night in the dusty recesses of their minds wake in the day to find that it was vanity: but the dreamers of the day are dangerous men, for they may act their dream with open eyes, to make it possible.

—T.E. Lawrence [Lawrence of Arabia]

In our time the destiny of man presents its meaning in political terms.

—Thomas Mann.

Ghana's Second Republic was based on the Westminster model and proceeded with the general election of August 29, 1969. The election was most exciting for the liberal democrats found themselves in the Progress Party led by Prof. K. A. Busia. Having spent many years in exile campaigning against Kwame Nkrumah and the CPP, he returned home with a big clout and a lot of money to finance his Party. The National Liberation Council (NLC) made him the Chairman of Civic Education, a position that enabled him to tour the country. Some said the NLC granted Busia an advantage over his opponents. Many of the critics of the military regime were also against the banning of the CPP from contesting the election, which meant that, the Progress Party had weak opposition from the smaller Opposition Parties that included The National Alliance of Liberals led by Kobla Agbeli Gbedema, The All People Republican Party led by E. V. C. de Graft Johnson, The United Nationalist Party led by H. S. Bannerman and The Peoples Action Party led by Imoro Ayarna.

In fact, the fact that Professor Busia was also seen as a friend of Akwasi Afrifa, one of the original coup leaders and a one time military Head of State (after the death of Joseph Ankrah), seemed to have made credible the criticism. Busia's Progress Party (PP) was therefore perceived to have won the elections on a silver platter. Notwithstanding the validity of the Opposition argument, it can still be said that the unpopularity of the Convention People's Party (CPP) which was demonstrated in the grand support for the coup leaders, made it unlikely for the CPP to be sent to power even if it had not been banned.

The Westminster type of Government that the new Constitution mandated was different from the Republican form of government presided over by Nkrumah. Edward Akuffo Addo, one time Chief Justice, became the ceremonial President. Other well-known political activists who had been in opposition to the CPP also assumed influential positions in the new constitutional Government. These included Victor Owusu, William Ofori Atta, and J.H. Mensah. Professor K.A. Busia was Prime Minister.

Not long after his swearing in ceremony, Prof. Busia sent the late Maxwell Owusu, who would later be appointed Asante Regional Minister, to talk to Kufuor and find out from him what he wanted to do in terms of membership in the new Government. Kufuor told Maxwell that he was interested in becoming the Minister of Local Government or Deputy Minister of Foreign Affairs. Maxwell returned later and informed the impatient Kufuor that the Prime Minister thought the Local Government Ministry was a bit too senior for him and that he would appoint him the Deputy Minister of Foreign Affairs. He was not yet 30 years but was excited because of one reason—Victor Owusu had been appointed the Minister of Foreign Affairs and he was going to work with him again.

Victor Owusu's influence on Kufuor had been really immense. Victor, in the opinion of Kufuor, was a workaholic and very thorough. Anybody who got close to him at the Bar would want to keep pace by also learning to be thorough.

A very meticulous gentleman, he was more often seen as controversial and even arrogant—a charge, which his biographer, the political scientist, Prof. E. Gyimah—Boadi disagrees with. Boadi rather argues that Victor Owusu was misunderstood and misinterpreted in his entire political life.

As Deputy Minister, Kufuor was supposed to learn the ropes. The management of the Foreign Affairs Ministry was exciting and Victor Owusu was really kind to him. He allowed him so much scope and entrusted him with important assignments. Kufuor was made to attend all the United Nations (U.N.) General Assembly meetings, Organization of Africa Unity (OAU) summits, Non-Aligned Movement conferences within the three years that the Progress Party was in power. Within two years, Kufuor had gotten to know a lot of personalities within the United Nations and befriended some of them.

He would sit around the table with about 36 Heads-of-State: world leaders like Tito (of Yugoslavia), Indira Ghandi (of India), Emperor Haile Selassie (of Ethopia) who did not hide their surprise at seeing such a young delegate from Ghana in their midst.

Mr. Diallo Telli, the Guinean first Secretary-General of the Organization of Africa Unity (OAU), became his personal friend and visited Kufuor anytime his travels brought him to Ghana. Every year, between 1969 and 71, Kufuor spent about a week in Addis Ababa taking part in the meetings of the OAU.

And Kufuor did really enjoy these diplomatic outings especially at the UN, where he would normally go a week before meetings. He would say:

> I felt that I was almost being professionalised as a diplomat under Victor.

The most spectacular event in which he was involved, was the 1971 debate on the seating of China at the U.N. Owusu had been moved from the Foreign Affairs Ministry to become Attorney – General and William Ofori Atta, a Cambridge University trained Economist, had replaced him. But because Owusu had established the tradition that every year Kufuor should go to the United Nations even if the substantive Minister would, which sometimes they did for short periods, Ofori Atta followed the tradition.

Kufuor, aided by the Ministry's civil servants would be entrusted with the actual work sessions.

It was as a result of this exposure that Kufuor read Ghana's statement about the seating of China and gave the vote.

The argument of Kufuor and for that matter the Government, which took a right-centre position, had been that while big China had to be admitted and seated within the Security Council, its coming should not exclude the retention of a seat in the General Assembly by Taiwan. Taiwan, at that time, had a population of over 14 million, which was bigger than that of Ghana, but it also had all the trappings of a State. The "ONE CHINA" argument did not influence Ghana's vote. The Government saw the whole situation as a history of multiple successions, and recognized the right of these two nations to re-unite in the future if, and when they chose to do so. Kufuor argued further that it was not the duty of outsiders to decide which should be and which should not be.

Of the three initial votes that were given, Ghana was the first country to do so, which later became the popular vote. China was eventually admitted to the U.N. and given the seat at the Security Council.

Not long after this, Prime Minister Busia, who was diabetic, suffered a bout of it and travelled to England for treatment. Whilst there, a group of military men led by Colonel I.K. Acheampong staged a coup that overthrew the PP Government. The soldiers constituted themselves into the National Redemption Council (NRC) and cited high inflation rate and the government's rural development policies, including the opening up of feeder roads to the villages, as some of the reasons for the military take-over.

The Government immediately arrested many of the leading figures including J.A. Kufuor. He was imprisoned for a year whilst others suffered over a year at Nsawam

Security Prison and other big prisons in the country.

When he was released, he engaged in a series of businesses. Kufuor knew that this hiccup was not the end of politics and that there would be another time to return to civilian rule. While he waited for that time, he had to work hard to make money. He had realized at that early stage, that politics was also about having money, so that the politician does not become the instrument of his financiers.

He initially went into business to export timber. Fortunately for him, an uncle who had an outfit in Takoradi was supportive and so soon, he gained some ground.

Concurrently, he partnered a tenant in one of his mother's houses in Kumasi, a Lebanese called Said and together, they formed a company called KUSAID. They distributed automotive batteries and also planned to set up a factory. Land was acquired at the Accra Industrial Area but along the line, they had some differences and so could not continue as planned.

Kufuor sold his shareholding and continued with the running of his other businesses, transport and a brick and tile factory — which he had established in Kumasi and Atiwama districts respectively.

But the return to civilian rule, which Kufuor had anticipated, was long in coming. Acheampong's Supreme Military Council which the NRC had become, had done worse than they accused the Busia regime of doing. The economy was bad, the standard of education fell and graduate unemployment went up. Shortage of food led to general petty trading to take advantage of the situation to create artificial scarcity of all goods and therefore, hike prices.

Corruption in Government was at the time unprecedented.

If the coup disrupted his political growth, it was in part a gain for his family. He had time to be with them and to supervise their growth.

All the five children enrolled at Christ the King School where they also attended (and still do) church.

John Kwarbo Kufuor like his father went to Prempeh College in Kumasi. Nana Ama Kufuor and the three others went to Achimota School.

In the early 1950s when Kufuor was growing up, it was not common for fathers or parents to be friendly with their children for fear of breeding contempt. He, however, created a very liberal family atmosphere in which his children were his friends and their friends, his friends. He visited them in boarding school and attended Parent- Teacher Association meetings. His love for them also became a big weakness. He found it difficult to offend them and even had to explain mild punishment, often in rebuke for their transgressions, when youthful aggression misled them.

Theresa was however the stabilizer to the over liberalized family atmosphere. She would be the one who would find everything wrong with the father allowing the children to attend late parties.

When they became young adults, especially Addo Kwarbo and Nana Ama, they did introduce their girlfriend and boyfriend to him and were recognized and accepted in the family.

As they grew into adulthood by the 1980s, they returned to Britain for further studies and remember very well, the early telegrams Dad would send on their birthdays.

In the sixth year of the military regime, in 1978, a palace coup led by General Frederick Akuffo, one of the closest of Acheampong's inner circles took place, resulting in the creation of the Supreme Military Council II, with Akuffo as the new Head of State whilst Acheampong suffered house arrest. Akuffo had argued that Acheampong had become recalcitrant to good reason and ignored the advice of all, including Joe Appiah who had lost out to

Busia in the Presidential election, but was drawn closer to the SMC I. The Supreme Military Council II was not different from the first one. The malaise continued. On June 4, 1979, a young military officer in his early 30s, Flt. Lt. J. J. Rawlings, led what was called the June 4 Uprising that overthrew the Akuffo Government.

Though a violent uprising, the action by the young officers had some popular support because of the messing up of the nation. The revolting soldiers executed by firing squad, three of Ghana's former Heads of State: Akwasi Afrifa, I.K. Acheampong, and Akuffo himself. Scores of other senior officers within the military and the police also perished.

The whole exercise, which Rawlings called "House-cleaning", lasted for three months, because the Akuffo Government was on the verge of transferring the country back to civilian rule. A time-table had been set and political parties were even campaigning when the uprising took place. Rawlings had assured the Nation that the time-table would be followed but the house-cleaning was critical.

On June 18, 1979, the parties were set for election. People, who still believed in the ideology of Nkrumah, had re-grouped to form the People's National Party (PNP) with Dr. Hilla Limann, who previously worked for the Ministry of Foreign Affairs, as its presidential candidate.

The Liberal Democrats, the Progress Party tradition of Prof. Busia, however found themselves in serious trouble. Two strong men of intellectual and social standing, Victor Owusu and William Ofori Atta—contested for the party leadership. Negotiations upon negotiations in Kumasi and Accra could not patch their differences, leading to a split. Victor Owusu led one side, the stronger side, Popular Front Party (PFP) and William Ofori Atta, popularly called Paa Willie, led the other side, United National Convention (UNC). There were other smaller parties and

44

independent candidates.

At the end of the elections, none of the candidates could get more than the 50% demanded by the Electoral Commission. Dr. Hilla Limann had 631,559 of the votes representing 35.32%, Mr. Victor Owusu had 533,928 representing 29.86%, Mr. William Ofori–Atta had 311,265 votes representing 17.41%, Col. Frank George Bernasko of the Action Congress Party had 167,775 votes representing 9.38% Alhaji Ibrahim Mahama of the Social Democratic Party had 66,445 representing 3.72% of votes. Dr. John Bilson of Third Force Party followed with 2.75% and the four independent candidates, Dr. R. P. Baffour, Messrs Kwame Nyanteh and Diamond Nii Addy with 0.49, 0.47, and 0.33 percent respectively. Alhaji Imoro Ayannah placed last with 0.27%. The split cost the tradition dearly, for the combined votes of the PFP and the UNC, was big enough to have cancelled the votes of the PNP. To be sure, the PNP leader, Dr. Hilla Limann, was unknown and untested. After graduation from the University of Ghana, he went to the London School of Economics and the University of Paris, Sorbonne. He was well educated, but not well-known.

A second round ballot for Dr. Limann and Victor was fixed for July 9, 1979, to determine who would get over 50 percent of the votes. Dr. Limann did, with 1,118,305 representing 61.98% with Victor Owusu obtaining 686,097 representing 38.02%.

J.A. Kufuor however won his parliamentary seat at Atwima on the ticket of the PFP and found himself on the Opposition bench in the Parliament of 1979.

The PFP became the main Opposition to Dr. Limann's Government, and to strengthen their position, entered into an alliance with the UNC and other smaller parties and independent MPs to form the All People's Party with Dr. John Bilson of The Third Force Party as leader.

Kufuor emerged as the Opposition Spokesman for Foreign Affairs and was listed by the second year, to become leader of the Party in Parliament through the prodding of Victor Owusu, who even though was not in Parliament, had his swathing clothes as a defeated candidate of the main Opposition.

But before all these democratic attempts, quarrels and misunderstanding associated with the game could crystallize into something positive, J. J. Rawlings, who had almost two years before handed over power to Dr. Limann, took it from him in another coup on December 31, 1981.

Kufuor had enjoyed Parliament so far, because the Opposition had been very resourceful and challenged the ruling Government, as any serious Opposition should. The economy was not in the best of shape but many Ghanaians did not see Limann as a dictator and would have preferred that he would be allowed to complete the four year mandate granted under the Constitution. This was, however, not to be for the youth of Dr. Limann's own party, eaten with Marxist rhetoric, had collaborated with Rawlings and the military, to overthrow the Government on ideological differences. The resulting Government was the Provisional National Defence Council (PNDC).

Their intention was to set up a Socialist State; a State that was in antagonism to all the aspirations of Western democratic culture, freedom of speech, dictation of the market and the encouragement of private sector development and wealth creation. Worst, was the culture of political murder and abduction of over three hundred prominent public figures, in the early stages of the Revolution.

Kufuor was not happy about the turn of events, for it unexpectedly diminished his hopes for the future and personal growth because he had by this time, decided to do no other work but participation in civilian politics.

If the waiting period during the Acheampong/Akuffo

SMC1 and II of six years were too long to bear, the Socialist State, under construction by Rawlings and the Provisional National Defence Council and its off-shoot, the National Democratic Congress, would take almost a generation—twenty years—to be history.

But Kufuor's relationship with Limann before and after his demise was polite. They first met in 1969 when Kufuor was Deputy Minister of Foreign Affairs and Dr. Limann was serving as an officer in Togo. Twice, when he went to that country for discussions with President Eyadema it was Dr. Limann who would do the French and English interpretation, since Kufuor did not speak French and President Eyadema did not speak English.

When fate tilted and Limann became President, he remembered his former Deputy Foreign Affairs boss and asked him, in the middle of 1980 to accompany him as Opposition spokesman of Foreign Affairs to an OAU summit in Freetown, Sierra Leone. This was truly an indication that the constitutional government of the Third Republic was civilian and worked, despite the economic problems of the period.

THE APAGYAFIE (Asante New Town-Kumasi)

President Kufuor's family house, where he grew up.

**Obaapanin Ama Ampoma (Nana Ama Dapaah),
Mother of President Kufuor (1903–1994)**

President Kufuor's wedding in the U.K. 1962

**President J. A. Kufuor after his call to the Bar
(1962)**

**President Kufuor during his practising days as a Lawyer
(1965)**

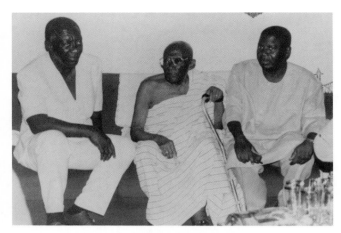

**L-R: President Kufuor, Baffour Osei-Akoto &
Vice President, Aliu Mahama (2001)**

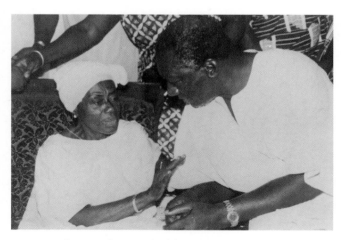

**President Kufuor with elder sister, Nana Durowaa
(2001)**

Prof. Adu Boahen, speaking at a Danquah-Busia Club
meeting. Behind him J.A. Kufuor (sitting), 1992

The late President of the Ghana Bar Association Mr. A.K.
Mmieh speaking at a Danquah-Busia meeting. Extreme
left: Dr. K. Addo Kufuor & right J.A. Kufuor (1992)

J.A. Kufuor with niece Gloria Prempeh (1960)

J.A. Kufuor voting (2000 elections)

**Arriving to be sworn into office
(January, 2001)**

**President Kufuor being sworn into office
(January, 2001)**

**President Kufuor delivering his inaugural address
(January, 2001)**

President Kufuor with his Ministers (2002)

**President Kufuor with a Chief on the mediation
team in the Yendi crisis (2002)**

**President Kufuor with Otumfuo Asantehene Osei Tutu II
(2002)**

President Kufuor on a Regional tour in Ghana (2001)

**President Kufuor with Laurent Gbagbo
during a visit to Ghana (2002)**

**President Kufuor with Kofi Annan UN Secretary General
(2002)**

**President Kufuor with Nigeria's President Obasanjo
(2002)**

President Kufuor with Senegal's President Wade (2001)

President Kufuor with British Prime Minister Tony Blair (2002)

**President Kufuor with French President Jacque Chirac
(2002)**

President Kufuor with HM Queen Elizabeth (2002)

**President Kufuor with Chinese President Jing Zeemin
(2002)**

President Kufuor with Pope John Paul (2002)

CHAPTER FIVE

Farewell to the Men on Horseback

Let us not seek scapegoats for the sins of yesterday, committed against Ghana; rather let us resolve never to permit ourselves to be fooled or bamboozled with empty slogans; Let us, here and now, never again to buy pigs in pokes but under God, "seek the truth, the way and the life" as one people with one destiny.

—Joe Appiah.

By 1990, it was obvious that the culture of silence, which had paralyzed political dissent in Ghana, had given way to political noise-making. In 1988, an eminent scholar who had retired from the University of Ghana, Prof. Albert Adu Boahen, had delivered the annual J.B. Danquah Memorial Lectures under the title: *The Ghanaian Sphinx: A Contemporary History of Ghana*, which had a bundle of criticisms against the dictatorship of J. J. Rawlings .The lectures set the country ablaze with agreements and disagreements about what the professor had to say, as he had quoted James Baldwin's *Fire Next Time,* to conclude. Many believed that the culture of silence was broken with the lectures.

Not long after, The Movement for Freedom and Justice (MFJ) was founded with Prof. Adu Boahen as Chairman. Executive Members included Johnny Hansen, Ray Kakraba Quarshie, the late Obeng Manu, Kwesi Pratt Jr., Dan Lartey, John Ndebugre, A. Owusu Gyimah and Akoto Ampaw. The MFJ was basically, a platform to resist the Rawlings dictatorship, canvass for the restoration of the fundamental rights of Ghanaians and the lifting of the ban on political activities.

In 1991, a veteran journalist, Attakorah Gyimah, Dr. John Bilson, Rev. Dr. Samuel Asante Antwi, then District Chairman of the Methodist Conference in Kumasi, Victor Owusu, Felicia Kufuor and other patrons that included Dr. Dsane Selby, founded another pressure group, Danquah-Busia Club, in Kumasi. The objective was to promote the political philosophy of Danquah and Busia, but, in the main, it was against the dictatorship of the Rawlings regime. It also canvassed for the restoration of multi-party democracy. This club, which became so popular, was attracting huge publicity in *The Pioneer* newspaper and negative publicity, with accusation of subversion against the government, by the State-controlled media.

It was clear by this time that it would not be long for party politics to resurface. The Provisional National Defence Council of J. J. Rawlings had itself, set up the National Commission for Democracy, under a former Judge — D.F. Annan. After the country tour of the Commission that started in Sunyani, Brong Ahafo region on July 5, 1990 ending on November 9, 1990, at Wa, Upper-West region, the consensus was that, Ghanaians were interested in party politics again.

Political organizations emerged that claimed to share Nkrumah's tradition. Among them were groups such as Our Heritage, Kwame Nkrumah Youngsters Club, Kwame Nkrumah Welfare Society and Kwame Nkrumah Foundation. All these groups claimed the promotion of the political ideas of Kwame Nkrumah, but in essence, they were political parties, waiting for the day when the ban on politics would be lifted, so that they could lawfully campaign for power.

J.A. Kufuor, seeing the signals of the return to party politics, resigned his post as Executive Chairman of the great Kumasi Asante Kotoko Football Club, a position he held for three years. He was not an executive member of the Movement for Freedom and Justice, although like all politicians at the time, he was a sympathizer. The MFJ had a very radical outlook and the executives even got arrested, (by the police under Government instruction), immediately after its inauguration in Accra but were later bailed. Many would later use it against Kufuor, that his inability to join radical groups to fight dictatorship itself, was a sign of his lack of leadership qualities.

The national executive members of the MFJ were made up of liberal democrats of the Danquah and Busia breed, and the group's socialist agitators including Kwesi Pratt and Akoto Ampaw who had been in prison several times, for opposing the Rawlings regime and for their association with the philosophies of Kwame Nkrumah.

Some of the Socialists in the PNP who helped to over-throw Dr. Limann, had become victims under Rawlings and had therefore joined the Opposition.

The first time Kufuor publicly identified with one of the clubs was at a Saturday meeting of the Danquah-Busia Club at K.O. Methodist School in Kumasi. He came with his brother, Kwame Addo Kufuor, to make a financial donation to the club. The Danquah-Busia platform was mainly for Rawlings bashing, unceasing insults and curs-es. Whereas such speakers received ovation, neither J.A. Kufuor nor his brother, could talk with such strong anger and in this sense, they became boring but their presence was highly recognized.

On the Monday after their maiden visit, *The Ghanaian Times* published a highly inflammatory report alleging that the Kufuor brothers had given out money for people to stage demonstrations in Kumasi and to overthrow the government. Though this was false, for the recorded pro-ceedings of the meeting as well as the many present at the gathering could attest to this, the newspaper report served notice to the country about what was going on in Kumasi. It also helped to attract many to the Danquah-Busia Satur-day meetings. In fact, this organization that started with about ten members present, had membership of about 1000 people eight months later.

Soon branches were opened in many parts of Kumasi and Brong Ahafo. While there were similar political gath-erings in Accra, Cape Coast and other places, the Kumasi meetings were by far, the best patronized. For the first time, many Nkrumahists like Nana Bediako Poku, for-mer General-Secretary of the CPP and diplomat, could speak freely on the platform of the Danquah-Busia organ-ization. Many, including Kufuor, travelled from Accra to Kumasi to spend their week-ends engaging in politics.

J.A. Kufuor was doing that at his mother's house where a lot of people would congregate to listen to him. By the end of 1991, when it became clear that the Danquah-Busia club would be turned into a political party the following year, the question of leadership emerged. Prof. Adu Boahen, because of his Danquah lectures, which boldly broke the "culture of silence," was emerging as the leader. In Kumasi, he was supported by the rich—Appiah Menka, Gyamfi Bikki—and the powerful. The bold men of the era including, Obeng Manu, thought that anybody who had had anything to do with Rawlings-in terms of accepting positions or appointments, had no business wanting to contest the presidential candidacy of the Busia-Danquah group. They were also agitators who thought Adu Boahen and only Adu Boahen, could confront Rawlings, should he decide to contest in the recently announced political election plans.

The era was certainly dictating its leadership. Kufuor had accepted a ministerial appointment from the military government of J.J. Rawlings when it overthrew the legitimate government of Dr. Hilla Limann. According to Kufuor, he did that on the advice of Victor Owusu, who suggested that three of his senior members in the Popular Front Party—Kufuor, Alhaji Mahama Iddrius and Dr. Obed Asamoah, should join the new government to control the excesses and as a form of national government. The explanation that evoked Victor Owusu's strategic advice did not do Kufuor any good. His eight-month service as PNDC Minister of Local Government, and 14 years after his resignation from that position, his perceived association with the military administration was still held against him by some. He had resigned in the wake of the murder of the three High Court judges (Mrs. Cecilia Koranteng Addo, Fred Poku Sarkodie, Justice G.A. Agyepong) and a retired army officer, Major Sam

Acquah. The incident referred to, marked a period of unprecedented judicial killings and disappearance of people in the history of Ghana. Though Kufuor argued that he only obeyed his party leadership by joining the military junta, no leader including Victor Owusu himself, came to his rescue or confirmed that the party indeed asked him to associate with the military.

Interestingly, some people were keen in the agitation against the Rawlings rule so much so that, even though Kufuor was trying to address issues of national concern some were not impressed. The most important statement, which also brought him the most criticism, was an interview he granted *Uhuru Magazine* in March 1992. The preface to the interview had described him as a "very likely choice (for presidential candidate) of the Danquah-Busia group". On top of that, he also gave some comments, which in the context of the interview, were representative of a political manifesto of his tradition's ideology.

Most opposition politicians never said anything nice about the Rawlings Government but in an answer to a question, Kufuor had been liberal:

> No doubt the past few years have recorded some stability and some economic revival, and naturally some of the credit, if not a substantial part of it should go to the PNDC Government. Why some of us accorded the PNDC only qualified credit was due to factors, numbered among which, included the following:
>
> The stability involved here is a forced one under the gun, and therefore, a false one that may not stand the test of time. The stability has not been generated from the inter change of view-points and ideas among the diverse and many forces composing the political spectrum of the nation.

Regular constitutionality with its acid test of accountability and probity chiefly on the part of the governors, has been totally absent over the entire period in question. The hallmark of the period has been an unbroken monologue by the regime, monopolizing all the official news media to the extent that the Head of State himself described it as "The Culture of Silence." The economic revival, to the man in the street, has been more of statistics than money in his pocket.

The first two years of the regime which were critical for the economy were wasted in "Revolutionary" posturing against the banks, the business community, and our creditors including the IMF and The World Bank; the USA and the Western capitalistic world in general. The regime did not know who its best friends were and therefore, flatly refused to talk to our creditors, and radically destroyed banking confidentiality, which seriously jeopardized the saving habit of the citizens of Ghana. Highly placed members of the regime are on record for questioning the relevance of devaluation to the national economic recovery. So eventually when the regime woke up to the necessity for devaluation, it resorted to the subterfuge of the "surcharge and bonus" policy, the wisdom and economics of which left very much to be desired. Doubtless, however, this policy worsened the status of the currency beyond doubt and must be blamed in no small measure for the thousand-fold devaluations the currency — the cedi — has been suffering ever since the government eventually came round and accepted to do things correctly. This it referred to as adjustment. Pronouncements from the "High Horse of Morality" by highly placed Government members against "corrupt" and "immoral" would-be foreign investors have also seriously frightened off much capital inflows. Also there is hardly any doubt that the regime has been very tardy in appreciating the role of the private sector in the Economic Recovery Process. It wasted a lot of time before trying to help with the development of native entrepreneurship. Indeed it undermined the little that there was.

This statement did not go down well with many of his critics. But who anointed Kufuor as the spokesman of the Danquah-Busia tradition? His spin-doctors however ensured that sections of this interview were used by some of the print media to spread the word but his opponents also went as far as to question the motive of the interviewer, Kojo Yankah.

By the end of 1991, factions of historical and contemporary colours had emerged within the Danquah-Busia Club. Historical because, Prof. Adu Boahen belonged to the United National Convention of 1979 which was headed by William Ofori Atta, and was indeed, rooted in the Danquah Busia tradition. J.A. Kufuor was, a stalwart of his old mentor, Victor Owusu, who also led the Popular Front Party. The two parties had split because of misunderstanding over leadership, a situation which prevented the Danquah-Busia tradition from winning over the Nkrumah party—People National Convention—headed by Dr. Hilla Limann. The Popular Front Party, tends to blame the UNC, and in particular, Adu Boahen, for subverting their chances of winning and there were political players of that era who were alive and wanted a revenge against the Professor. So Kufuor's support base was from this group of influential past players. But there were others within the same group who were also pushing another contestant, a medical doctor — Kofi Dsane Selby. Selby, like Kufuor, belonged to the PFP sector of the Danquah-Busia tradition and came from the Central Region of Ghana though he had lived all his life in Kumasi and practiced medicine there. He served in the diplomatic service as Ghana's Ambassador to France under Busia.

Another figure to emerge, not so much because of political pedigree but business establishment, was J.A. Addison also from the Central Region and former President of the Ghana Association of Industries

Whilst all these were going on, another prominent member of the Danquah-Busia tradition, Dr. Kwame Safo Adu, was in prison on serious charges of economic crime against the State. Accused by the Government of defrauding the IMF and the World Bank, Rawlings himself flew, one Saturday morning, to Kwamo near Kumasi where Dr. Safo Adu's pharmaceutical industry had been set up and closed it down. If he was found guilty of any of the over ten charges, he would be imprisoned for life or hanged. His trial, which was of international business importance and a test for international development and direct investment, had arrested the attention of the nation. When the verdict set Safo Adu free, it became a moral victory, which propelled him to contest the presidency. Dr. Safo Adu had been in the Busia Government of 1969-71 and served as Minister of Agriculture.

An unknown lawyer, Kwame Kodua, caused a stir when he also decided to join the race for the party's leadership. From Kumasi, he told a press conference that he had had a vision from God in which he was directed to contest for the presidency and that he would win. He preached the word of God throughout his campaign and never told his listeners what he would do for the party and the nation if he should be elected.

When the ban on political activities was lifted, the

NPP would be the first to have a congress to elect party leaders for the upcoming national presidential and parliamentary elections, which the government had fixed for December 1992. The incumbent military government had played all sorts of tricks up to this point. This point was attested to in an interview this author had with Prof. Adu Boahen on the issue of Constitutional Process and Referendum in Ghana on August 1, 1991. The subject and its responses became an MFJ working paper. In the said interview, Prof. Boahen lamented thus:

> In a series of memoranda, press statements and at various symposia and public lectures, we have called for the convening of constitutional conference to draw up the modalities and the time table for the transitional process, the establishment of an elected Constituent Assembly to draw up and promulgate a Constitution for the Fourth Republic, the resignation of the PNDC and the setting up of an interim government to oversee the transitional process, the dissolution of the National Commission for Democracy which is PNDC—created and dominated institution and its replacement by an independent Electoral Commission to conduct the election involved in the whole transitional process, and finally for the lifting of the ban on political parties.
>
> Unfortunately, the PNDC has treated all these demands, but two of them, with utter contempt. Instead of convening a constitutional conference to work out the details of the transitional process in a democratic manner, the PNDC has arbitrarily decided to set up a nominated Committee of Experts and a Consultative, rather than a Constituent Assembly, to prepare a Constitution for

the Fourth Republic.

Secondly, the PNDC has persistently refused to announce even a time-table for the transmission to constitutional civilian rule. To this date, therefore, nobody knows when the Constitution being drafted will be promulgated, when the general elections will be held and when the transfer of power will take place.

Thirdly, the PNDC has to date refused to repeal the repressive laws. Some independent newspapers like *The Catholic Standard* remains banned while the entire public media, the radio, television and the two state owned newspapers, *The People's Daily Graphic* and *The Ghanaian Times*, the only mass-circulation newspapers in the country, are rigidly controlled by the PNDC and no access whatsoever, is given to the pro-democracy and other anti-PNDC forces in the country.

All the numerous press statements, press conferences, lectures and symposia issued or held by the MFJ and the other bodies are hardly ever mentioned in the mass media. The sad result is that to this day, most of us have to tune in to the *BBC* and *Voice of America* or read the weekly *West Africa* published in London, to get real information about the events and activities in the country.

August 1992 was fixed for the NPP Congress at the University of Ghana, Legon. By this time, many other papers had hit the newsstands. Hitherto, the PNDC had passed a "licensing law" that banned unofficial newspaper. Some of the nation's journalists working for the private media suffered humiliation, unemployment, and even murder. When the ban on the press was lifted, many of these writers sought revenge against the PNDC. Papers

like *Young and Old, The Christian Chronicle, The Ghanaian Chronicle* and *The Vanguard* became anti-PNDC.
Many of these newspapers found in Professor Adu Boahen, the symbol of the crusade against the PNDC regime,
and the days leading to the Congress were inundated with
publications and editorials on the contestants.

J.A. Kufuor had also emerged as the Professor's main
challenger. The two other key positions to be contested at
the Congress were for the Chairmanship of the party and
that of the General Secretary. It was obvious who would
win. Mr. B. J. da Rocha, an eminent lawyer and teacher,
had emerged as the father of the PFP side of the Danquah-
Busia tradition. He supported Kufuor and so was the late
Agyenim Boateng, who served in the Busia government of
1969 and was Secretary of the PFP in 1979. Kufuor's
strength in the coming election were his good looks,
diplomatic countenance and support from some of the
old people in the party. He also publicised the fact of his
experience in politics, being a Deputy Minister of Foreign
Affairs in his 30s and serving under two of the nation's
most illustrious Foreign Ministers, Victor Owusu and
William Ofori Atta as well as being the former Member of
Parliament for Atwima Nwabagya. His political credentials also included an award of an International Visiting
Fellowship which allowed him to travel through over
twenty states within the United States. Indeed, it was on
this tour that he met many leading politicians and
befriended some, like George Bush, Jr., later President of
the United States.

Still, he was not very popular among the Electoral
College in his home base Asante. A warrior people histor-
ically, they had come to see the fight to unseat Rawlings as
one demanding bravery, which Kufuor had not shown in
the anti-Rawlings posturing. Kufuor's support base had
been in the three northern regions of Ghana and   espe-

cially among the Dagombas.

Also, because of an ancient belief of Asante's aggression for power and an imperialistic past, some Ghanaians were never at easy with a possible Asante president. And the fact that five of the NPP presidential candidates were Asantes did not allay these fears. This did not help Kufuor's cause. In fact, an anti-Asante slogan—"anybody but an Asante" had emerged, arguing that because of that perception—the party should seek other candidates. Some of his own Asante people, who did not respect his leadership qualities if they thought he had any at all, started this campaign.

Adu Boahen, on the other hand, had had little experience in politics other than his brave criticism of undemocratic Ghanaian regimes. Born in 1932, he received his Ph.D from the School of Oriental and African Studies of the University of London and taught history at the University of Ghana for over twenty years. He was also the Dean of Graduate Studies. A distinguished African historian, he has published several books and papers on Africa. He was once President of the Historical Society of Ghana and Secretary of the Ghana Academy of Arts and Sciences as well as the President of The International Scientific Committee of UNESCO responsible for the preparation and publication of its eight volumes on Africa history. Professor Boahen became the first Ghanaian to win the Noma Award with his non-fiction book, *The Centenary History of Mfantsipim School.* His political criticism started with his many articles against Kwame Nkrumah's perceived dictatorial tendencies, especially his introduction of the Preventive Detention Act. After the overthrow of the Busia Government by General I.K. Acheampong, Prof. Boahen delivered a strong critique of the military before going underground. He was very active in political demonstrations against the Acheampong regime and was a member of the People's Movement for Freedom and Justice that opposed Acheampong's Supreme Military Council.

However, when he stood for parliamentary election at Juaben in 1979, he lost. When he retired from the University of Ghana in 1985 after failing to secure the Vice Chancellorship position, a post which many people at the University agreed he was due and which many political friends expressed sympathy when the government manipulated the process for his non-appointment, Adu Boahen went to the United States to teach for some time.

When the time came for politics, those who were on the side of Kufuor and knew that the Professor was eminently qualified for the Vice Chancellorship, still declared him "a failure" unqualified for leadership.

Indeed, Adu Boahen himself was not very keen on the political leadership, as he did not oppose the Rawlings regime nor did he decide to deliver the Danquah Lectures, as a prelude to that Government's removal. At least, that was the impression he created. But as he continued to lead the Opposition Movement, he was unconsciously building political confidence in the minds of the people. It took some lobbying from people including chiefs in the Asante region, before it dawned on the Professor to contest for the political leadership of the party. Once his mind was made up and he started drawing the crowds to his functions, he became intoxicated with party politics. Adu Boahen's popularity notwithstanding, Kufuor stayed in the contest. However, he arranged with the new parliamentary candidate for the Atwima District, James Adusei Sarkodie, that should the decision for the presidential candidacy not go well, Kufuor would return to contest the parliamentary seat of his old district. This was an agreement that would later serve Kufuor well.

On the eve of elections, there were serious negotia-

tions with some members of the electoral college. Some
had changed camp, and there were also painful betrayals
from some of Kufuor's trusted friends from Asante and
the North.

Victor Owusu, Kufuor's long time mentor, was ill in
London and had failed to endorse him. Whether Owusu,
who still had tremendous respect could have changed the
opinion of the voters, is still not clear.

The congress had been fixed to take place from August
27-29. The date was chosen to coincide with the four-
teenth anniversary of the death of Prof. K.A. Busia, (who
passed away on August 28, 1978, at his home in Stand-
lake, 12 miles from Oxford where he had lived since his
overthrow). The morning of August 27 was used to pay
tribute and songs of praises in his name. On August 29,
1992, many supporters of the Danquah-Busia tradition
arrived in Accra from all parts of Ghana, to elect their
party officers and presidential candidate. Two thousand
people in all, that is ten people from each of the two hundred constituencies of the country, constituted the electoral college. The crowd at the University of Ghana at
Legon was however, over ten thousand. The tradition had
officially adopted the name—New Patriotic Party—
with the Elephant as its symbol. They had failed to use the
name Progress Party, after losing a court case that reinforced the ban on the use of old party names, after the military take-over in December 1981. Many of the youthful
supporters who went to Legon had not seen a party congress before. There was great excitement and supporters of
all the seven candidates wore T-shirts bearing the pictures
of the candidates; balloons floating in the air, brass band
music flowing all night. Though it was becoming clear
that Adu Boahen would win, it was not so clear by how
many numbers or whether there would even be a run off.

After the opening of the Congress in the morning, and

the state of the party addresses, followed by solidarity messages from the other parties, the candidates were introduced. Each candidate had a nominee to introduce him, and that was strategic, for the more famous the person, the better.

Prof. Adu Boahen had Dr. Jones Ofori Atta introduce him. A leading Ghanaian economist, Ofori Atta had been Deputy Minister for Finance under the Busia Government. He had also taught Economics at the University of Ghana, and was one of the heroes who had recently returned from exile in Uganda, where he served as the Governor of that country's Central Bank. He could have qualified to contest as presidential candidate, but decided to support Prof. Adu Boahen. In his endorsement, Ofori Atta stressed Adu Boahen's virtues as freedom fighter, and one who risked his life to challenge "the evil regime of the Rawlings dictatorship, when others were dining with the regime" (an obvious reference to Kufuor's short tenure as Minister of Local Government). The Professor's stature as an international scholar was also mentioned. Being a far better speaker than the Professor himself, many believed that Dr. Ofori Atta's speech changed the minds of some delegates at the Congress in Adu Boahen's favour.

Dr. Kwame Safo Adu had also strategically chosen Courage Quarshigah, a cousin of Rawlings, who had just been released from prison on an alleged plot to overthrow the regime. Equally a good talker, and a very prominent and respected Ewe soldier, he did justice by arousing the sympathies of the delegates for Safo Adu. So did the speakers for Dr. Dsane Selby, Kwame Kodua and Dr. Addison.

Kufuor however, was to absorb a shock when at the last moment, one of his trusted friends who was to do the introduction, indicated that he would not be able to do so. Obviously, he had shifted to another camp. A volunteer — an old boy of Prempeh College, eventually performed the role. Commenting on the development, Kufuor reflected:

> My opponents just wanted to dislocate me radical-
> ly but somehow, they did not succeed so those who
> had been chosen to do that, disappointed me.
>
> I wish I could tell you why they were so much
> against me. A lot of explanations were given. Some
> attacked me because I am an Asante; others
> thought I am Victor Owusu's protégée and as you
> know, Victor was always seen as a controversial
> politician. Others perhaps out of personal dislike. I
> thought I knew myself best or better than anybody
> could know me, and I had the staying power or
> what it would take, to challenge.

After midnight, the votes were counted. The Professor
emerged the winner with 1,121 votes representing 56.6 %
of total votes; Kufuor tipped to place second, had placed
third with 326 votes representing 16.5%, having been
overtaken by a less fancy candidate, Dr. Kofi Dsane Selby,
with 343 votes representing 17.3%, followed by Dr.
Kwame Safo Adu with 149 votes representing 7.5%, Dr.
John Atta Addison followed him with 32 votes representing 1.6% and John Kwame Kodua 9 votes representing
0.5% The atmosphere was electrifying. The Adu Boahen
supporters were beside themselves with joy for the victory. After pledges from the losers to support the Professor,
the delegates travelled in the night to their constituencies.

There was an arrangement that the following morning, Sunday, all the losers will accompany the presidential
candidate elect, to the Christ the King Church for the
Thanksgiving Service. Surprisingly, the only loser who
mustered courage with beaming smiles to accompany
Prof. Adu Boahen, was J. A. Kufuor. The other candidates, either out of the stupor of shock or exhaustion,

could not go.

J.A. Kufuor returned to his earlier arrangement to stand as the MP for Atwima, as James Adusei Sakordie stepped down for him. The party had still not completed nomination for candidates. An old horse in the constituency, and not affected by the upset, Kufuor set about organizing again for parliamentary nominations on 10th November.

But the time between the NPP election of their leader and the general election gave them only seven months to contest nationally. Though the campaign began in earnest across the towns and villages in the country, it was clear that there was not sufficient time, money and logistics for the party to compete with the incumbent military Government, which had become a political party and adopted the name, National Democratic Congress (NDC). It had the Umbrella as its symbol, and Ft. Lt. J. J. Rawlings, the uncontested and unopposed presidential candidate.

Prof. Adu Boahen, who had won the party's election with a promise to prosecute the Rawlings regime and to put to trial, many of them for human rights abuses and corruption, had raised the political temperature so high that, there was tremendous tension in the air. Coming from a liberal democratic tradition, his campaign theme was based on the interests of the property-owning class, and a promise to promote private enterprise development. An attempt to form an alliance, (against the incumbent Government), with the smaller opposition parties, Peoples' National Convention (PNC) headed by former President Dr. Hilla Limann, Convention People's Party (CPP) by Emmanuel Erskine, and the Peoples' Convention Party (PCP) of Kwabena Darko, had failed mainly because of ideological differences. Above all, there was not enough time for compromises on major and minor details of such an alliance.

As the days approached for the elections, the private

press went heavily against the incumbent Government. *The Independent* newspaper then edited by Kabral Blay Amihere, who had just returned to Ghana as a Nieman Fellow from Harvard University, endorsed the candidacy of Prof. Adu Boahen, a novelty that drew protest from the Press Secretary of the NDC, Vincent Assiseh. *The Ghanaian Chronicle* edited by another good and aggressive journalist, Nana Kofi Coomson, in a survey also predicted that the Professor was going to win by almost 60 percent of the votes, to avoid a re-run. Even die-hard CPP activists and former Ministers of Nkrumah's Government including Mr. F. A. Jantuah, held press conferences in Kumasi to urge people to vote for Professor Adu Boahen. The Professor, by these developments, had become sure of his victory. Even foreigners, who happened to be in the country at the time, thought the same.

A week before the elections, I went with an American historian, Jean Allman to Kumasi to see the Professor, at the heavily guarded home of one of his financiers, Appiah Menka. The Professor was about to address selected parliamentary candidates for the party, which included J.A. Kufuor, happily mingling with his colleagues.

"Well, I thought I should come and pay my last respect to you before you become the President of the Republic of Ghana." Allman told the Professor in the still heavy security presence.

There were even rumours, later debunked by the campaign team, that a cabinet list had even been prepared in anticipation of victory.

But whilst the Professor made these bold tours of the country in cohort convoys, the incumbent President Rawlings was sometimes flying to towns and cities in the company of District Chief Executives, Regional Ministers and other state functionaries, using state machinery including money, to bankroll the NDC campaign. The

Opposition parties were clearly at a disadvantage. They were not sure of how long the urban anti-Rawlings feelings would last. They also believed that the Electoral Commission was not independent, and that the Voters Register, had been inflated with the names of paid agents tasked to increase the number of voters in Rawlings' favour. Despite these odds, the Opposition believed that it could win the elections.

The Great Depression, was unfortunately how *The Ghanaian Chronicle* reported the elections, the morning after on November 4, 1992, which saw the Professor surprisingly losing by a large margin to Rawlings. Rawlings had obtained 2,323,135 votes representing 58.4 percent; followed by Adu Boahen, with 1,204,764 votes representing 30.3 percent with Dr. Hilla Limann of PNC collecting 266,710 representing 6.7 percent. Kwabena Darko collected 113,629 votes representing 2.9 percent and the last, General Emmanuel Erskine, 69,827 representing 1.8 percent.

Professor Adu Boahen, who had voted in Accra and rushed up to Kumasi went back again to Accra, to hold a press conference to speak up against the results. He accused the Government of rigging the elections. Adu Boahen would later express his and others thoughts, in the book, *The Stolen Verdict.* It recorded the details of how the elections were rigged with data and evidence from all over the country.

The parties also argued that they would not participate in the parliamentary elections until a "traditional authority was established to supervise, among other things, the electoral process; a completely new voters register was compiled and identity cards issued to voters; the interim National Electoral Commission, which conducted the presidential election, was replaced by a new Commission whose members would include representatives of the competing political parties."

This notwithstanding, the fact that the international observers from The Commonwealth Observer Mission, Carter Centre from Atlanta, United States, and other independent observers, who the Opposition had insisted should witness the election gave it a fair result label, generated some controversy of the Opposition stand.

In the midst of this allegation of a rigged election, uneven electoral field, bloated electoral register, over exploitation of incumbency, the question was whether or not the NPP and the other opposition parties, would participate in the forthcoming parliamentary elections. The NPP was divided on this issue. There was the Kufuor faction, that argued that for the sake of democracy, they should contest and even as minority, act as a check on the Government which by the election results, would also dominate parliament. The other faction, Pro-Adu Boahen, argued that if the electoral register was over-bloated to suit the incumbent Government, and the election was rigged as the Pro-Kufuor faction generally accepted, what would be the sense in absorbing another calculated humiliation?

Because the Adu Boahen faction was in the majority, and popular sentiment countrywide was on their side, the Opposition boycotted the election. Insiders of the NPP organization argue that popular sentiment aside, the boycott was a deliberate plan to frustrate Kufuor, who his opponents in the party acknowledged, had comported himself well, supported Adu Boahen's efforts throughout, but who, if the party should go to Parliament, would eventually emerge as the leader of the Opposition and therefore overshadow Prof. Adu Boahen. For as a defeated presidential candidate, he had no executive role to play in the Party and in Parliament.

And so the NPP had to wait for another two years

before it could decide whether to elect another presidential candidate or not for the 1996 elections.

CHAPTER SIX

Waiting for Godot

There are two kinds of leaders. There is the man or woman who creates the self, his or her life, out of the drive of personal ambition, and there is the man or woman who creates a self out of response to peoples' need. To the one, the drive comes narrowly from within; to the other, it is a charge of energy that comes of others' needs and the demands these make.

—Nadine Gordimer.

Article 129(1) of the New Patriotic Party Constitution says, "the election of the party's presidential candidate shall take place at a National Congress held not later than twenty-four months from the date of the national election .The date and the venue for the National Congress shall be decided by the National Council, provided however that the National Council may on appropriate occasion vary the date." This was the hub!

Having agreed that the 1992 national election was rigged and hence *The Stolen Verdict*, supporters and spin-doctors of Prof. Adu Boahen, argued that it was not necessary for the party to have another congress but rather, maintain the Professor, since the defeat of the party was not for lack of the Professor's marketability. Apart from that, as an opposition party, the NPP lacked the resources with which to organize another congress in 1994. What is worst, the competition to select a presidential candidate was so straining that its aftermath, led to animosity among supporters and the competitors, creating instability in the party.

Of course, Prof. Adu Boahen would want to protect his status, for uncertainties lie deep in such contest. With an electoral college of only two thousand people, whose allegiances could always be unreliable, and whose votes could be swayed, sometimes by how much money a candidate has for his campaign, and how they themselves benefited, prevention was the best cure.

But for the other candidates, especially J.A. Kufuor, who had the ambition to try again, the argument did not wash. If a democratic party would not obey its own Constitution then, what was the guarantee that they would be able to protect the national Constitution? On top of that, there is nowhere in the Constitution that addressed the above argument concerning rigged elections in favour of an incumbent presidential candidate.

It was a situation of law versus morality. But morality, a Supreme Court Judge in Ghana, Bamford Addo says, does not matter in law and that was really the situation the NPP found itself in.

Beyond this, the two factions started testing the arguments on their supporters. Party platforms became avenues where the leading figures congregated for espousing these opposed views and casting innuendoes.

Prof. Adu Boahen had, as usual, popular support. For a party that had suffered serious leadership crisis since its birth in the 1940s, this was disturbing to the supporters. He had also become sentimental and according to party insiders, dictatorial. When Nana Akuffo Addo, who was his Campaign Director, crossed with him and decamped, it became clear that the accusation had some substance. When Dr. Amoako Tuffuor another campaign team member decamped, the media were interested in investigating accusations of dictatorship and there were signs of evidence. When some of the evidence were published, the media were accused of being on the payroll of the other faction, specifically the Kufuor side, but these did not diminish the popularity of the Professor.

The Professor's trump card against Rawlings had been that, he was the only person, who could stand up to him. Having lost the 1992 elections, and now at the age of 62, some questioned the vigour with which he could contest again.

At a rally in December 1994 in Kumasi, Prof. Adu Boahen himself backed out, and said his earlier argument of no election was unfair, and that he would prefer a party congress, because he was very sure he would win.

Within the same month, these squabbles and disagreements had created more factions. The Patriotic Club, a supposedly foot-soldier organization, emerged to galvanize party organization at the grassroots. An attempted inauguration of the Club, failed, at the Cultural Centre in Kumasi. The Regional Secretariat of the party denounced the Club publicly, and accused it of being anti-NPP.

It was in the midst of this confusion that Nana Ama Paa, Kufuor's mother, died at 90. She had seen a lot happen, and had supported Kufuor morally and financially, in his campaign to win the party's presidency in 1992. She also died proud of the family heritage. In an animated interview, she told Jean Allman in 1984 of how Francis Kufuor, her eldest son obtained Professor Emeritus status, at the Kwame Nkrumah University of Science and Technology.

The funeral was a durbar. It saw in attendance the only living ex-president, the late Dr. Hilla Limann. Victor Owusu, Kufuor's mentor and Popular Front Party presidential candidate as well as three other presidential candidates — Prof. Adu Boahen, General Erskine and Kwabena Darko — also attended. These people came with senior colleagues, political courtiers, praetorian characters and former Ministers and Secretaries of State. The Parliamentary Minister, J.H. Owusu Acheampong, led the Government side. Interestingly, it was at this funeral that a public announcement, denying the Club, was made by the Asante Regional Secretariat that had as Chairman, Dr. Kwame Donkor Fordwor and Secretary A.K. Korankye. Posters had however been distributed, announcing the birth of the Club. Its promoters, Dr. Dsane Selby, Dr. Wereko Brobby, Colin Essamuah, Dr. Wayo Seini and Dr. Nyaho Tamakloe, were to become the Club's watch dogs against what it called, "indiscipline and bribery at the party's local election." Opponents within the party, however, described it as a conscious or unconscious usurpation, of the party's peace by its own fundamentalists.

Conceived days after the Asante Regional election, which elected Dr. Donkor Fordwor as Chairman amidst

controversy of vote buying, it had as its motto "commitment without inducement" and had as members, some of
the losers of the regional executive party election in
Kumasi—mainly Kufuor supporters.

Of course, this was a careful Kufuor group. Though he
would deny this later, the fact that meetings were held in
Apagyafie, and the supporters were mainly Kufuor fans
that met with him for discussions during his weekly visits,
to Kumasi confirmed this. He would later make a diplomatic statement on this: "So long as such a Club, (Patriotic Club), would not break up the party, but rather, intend
to introduce a sort of discipline to remind us of the chief
aims of the party, it could be accommodated…these days
the temptation to fall prey to money is so strong, and
whereas, one would not deny the importance in the rally-
ing of parties, the moral principles supporting such formation, would be undermined, if a stop is not put to
using money as the main determination in politics."

By this, Kufuor tacitly condemned alleged corruption
through proxy, a style that would be seen in many difficult
situations.

The opponents of this Club, of course, included Prof.
Adu Boahen, Appiah Menka, Dr. Kwame Donkor Ford-
wor and some executives of the Asante Secretariat. A.K.
Korankye, the Secretary commented at the time:

> The Secretariat is not against any group that wants
> to mobilize support for the NPP but the activities
> of this Club are suspicious and inconsistent with
> the Constitution of the party. For apart from hav-
> ing a different logo, there are secret meetings
> attended only by invitation.

The most senior member of the Patriotic Club, Dr.
Dsane Selby, responded to me this way, at the time:

How can anybody in his right senses, believe that we can be for a club opposed to the party we belong? The NPP has been accused and rightly so of not having strong roots in the rural areas though we have wards and other facilities there. We admitted this, and felt the need to form a club and get dedicated young men who love the party, and train them to go to the rural areas to promote the party....

We have the Young Executive which mobilizes money for the Party. We have COMO with Charles Appiah as Co-coordinator. Why is it that if another organ is to be formed with certain people, it should be seen as subversion?

Interestingly, the COMO was another group formed as a lobby to promote the interest of Prof. Adu Boahen. Charles Appiah, a very close associate of the Professor was its co-ordinator. Thus, no matter whatever accusation people were making it was for a purpose. Apart from Asante, other regions were calmed.

The Asante region has the bulk of the party's national support. In the 1992 election, over 70 percent of the people voted NPP. It had the biggest voting population nation-wide and the highest number of parliamentary constituencies, 33. Whichever candidate had the bulk of the region's support was therefore half-way through, and whichever party also had the region's support, was confident. It was sort of a strategic region where all the candidates, interestingly based in Accra, would travel to every week-end.

By October 1994, the NPP had not fixed a date for congress let alone, elect a leader. They had argued in the 1992 election that their inability to elect a leader earlier so that campaign could follow, was one of the reasons of their defeat but still, they delayed. The foot-dragging was strategic, for by this time, Professor Adu Boahen had virtually clashed with the national executives of the party, and they would prefer any of his opponents winning. Yet, he was still popular. To go to Congress, was to meet the likely event of his being re-elected. To delay, would possibly help his opponents. Desperate, because of these internal politics, the Professor started to make serious allegations against some of his opponents, out of anger rather than of substance. He even accused Kufuor of bribing the electoral college, an accusation that he had to later retract, when the NDC used the same statement against the NPP. It was also said by the Professor's inner group, that it was an accusation planted in the media, by his detractors to incur more displeasure for him.

As the Editor of *The Ashanti Independent*, I commissioned I.K. Gyasi, a seasoned political writer to contribute a piece in the October 3, 1994 edition titled, AND TO THE OPPOSITION. And this was what he had to say:

> Of course I have written before on the chances of the National Democratic Congress (NDC) and the Opposition Parties in the 1996 General Elections.
>
> However, with the pathetic showing of the Opposition Parties at the most, I feel my observation at the time can still bear repeating, hence this article.
>
> The NDC already has a leader, President Rawlings, and he has announced with cocky assurance that beating the Opposition in 1996 would be such an easy task that the party should rather think of how to combat poverty and other socio-economic ills that plague the country.
>
> What can we say of the NPP, which appears to be relatively the strongest of the Opposition Parties?
>
> As I have observed before, the NPP is riddled with factionalism.

Apart from the clearly discernible anti and pro-Adu Boahen, there are also sub-factions, each one with a leader having   presidential ambitions.

By this time, the NPP should have made known to the electorate who the presidential aspirant is so that the electorate may get to know him well before 1996.

Instead, one sees nothing but an unseemly bickering and jockeying for leadership right in the open, instead of behind closed doors.

Everyone's knife is out, not against the NDC but against one another.

I have said it before, but let me repeat that one of the problems of the NPP, which is a hang-over from its ancestor parties, is a congenital inability to suppress big egos.

I know that the NPP would reply that theirs is a democratic party in which no decisions are imposed on members.

Do not believe them, for it would be a mere rationalization of a congenital defect.

There is no doubt that a national congress will be held and a presidential candidate will eventually be chosen but the present state of affairs is doing the party no good at all.

One has to admit that no matter how well prepared a boxer is, a crooked decision can rob him of victory.

In Black Africa where "sit-tight" presidents abound, one should not rule out shady practices by the party in power to hang on to power.

The party or parties in opposition therefore have every reason to expect flagrant or subtle breaches of the law in order to ensure victory.

But it is equally true that a boxer who goes into

the ring only half prepared will be clobbered into defeat without any crooked officials having to give the fight to his opponent.

What state of preparedness can the NPP claim to be in at the moment?

I have concentrated on the NPP because, of all the Opposition Parties, it is the only one that can show a fair promise of giving the NDC a fight to ensure that party political democracy truly works in this country....

I. K. Gyasi's article also produced its critics. But whilst the fears of a possible split in the NPP ran deep, J.A. Kufuor thought it somehow normal in an interview with me in *The Ashanti Independent:*

We should pick our candidate with about a year and a half to the election...one will not be sincere with oneself if one didn't admit that there seems to be traces of the unfortunate split in the ranks of the NPP. But I want to stress the word "traces."

I will say in all honesty, that the two factions have learnt some lessons from 1979. What is happening now is   perhaps what will be described as evidence of the second nature of the human beings concerned...

By January 1995, the National Council, a Council made up of members who have given of their best and have contributed significantly to the formation, welfare and progress of the Party, decided that the election of the presidential candidate should take place in March, 1996.

This did not rest the issue. On August 26, 1995, the party had its 4th Annual National Delegates Conference at the University of Ghana. The two thousand people endorsed the date for the congress to elect presidential candidate in 1996. They also pushed the party into a new phase. Mr. da Rocha, the old man of the party was retiring. A new Chairman and a new executive were to be elected.

Again, the Pro-Kufuor and Pro-Adu Boahen factions were at work. It was a test to also check their popularity. Even other contestants were still leaning toward one of the two factions of the party.

Peter Ala Adjetey, a Constitutional Lawyer and former MP, was one of the candidates for the Chairmanship contest. He was supported by some Pro-Kufuor delegates, and also some Adu Boahen supporters, and eventually won. He had played a sort of a   neutral role to get the support of the two factions, though his sympathies were with Adu Boahen. Like him, Adjetey belonged to the UNC divide of 1979, and even though he was for Adu Boahen, he was seen as moderate.

Agbalno Wosi became the Vice Chairman; Salifu Bawa Deyaka became the first Vice Chairman with Ama Busia as the Second Vice Chairman. The late Agyenim Boateng, who was sometimes pro-Kufuor, and sometimes pro- Adu Boahen, managed to maintain his position. Hackman Owusu Agyeman became the Treasurer.

The new executives were slightly pro-Kufuor or at least, not strongly anti-Kufuor, though this would itself not be a strong factor.

By January 1996, a new concept had developed. Without an alliance of all the Opposition forces, the NPP could not win. A group of radical "youth" that included politicians of all ideological shades—Nana Akuffo Addo, Dr. Wereko Brobby, Dr. Nyaho Tamakloe, Victor Newman, Akoto Ampaw, Kwesi Pratt, Kwaku Baako and others, had formed an Alliance for Change, to challenge through unprecedented mass demonstrations, the "abuse of human rights and electoral fraud of the NDC Government". The success of these demonstrations against the Government's introduction of a tax system called Value Added Tax (VAT) and the fact that the Opposition group outside Ghana, led by intellectuals like George Ayittey of American University, had made it clear that without an Alliance of opposition forces to contest the up-coming 1996 elections, they were not going to continue contributing money or moral support. But the Alliance for Change itself, collapsed around the heads of Nana Akuffo Addo and Dr. Wereko Brobby, whose struggle to lead the Alliance reminded one of Trotsky and Lenin as they both rushed home to Russia on the eve of the great October 1917 Revolution, to take up the leadership. Trotsky was travelling from North America by ship and Lenin from Europe by train. Nana Addo, like Lenin, took over the leadership, because he got the votes of the other executives on time.

Another well-known Economist whose past experience included working for the United Nations, had emerged on the NPP scene. Kwame Pianim, a Yale University graduate, had made very dispassionate economic analysis on both radio and TV and was certainly loved by the media. His intention, put the Kufuor and Adu Boahen campaign in jeopardy, in terms of freshness of appeal. But he had a problem that needed a court interpretation; his involvement in an attempt in the 1980s to violently overthrow the Rawlings regime, landed him in prison on treason charges. He thus carried an ex-convict tag. When all the arrangements had been made for the Congress, the High Court ordered its postponement for Pianim's eligibility or otherwise to be cleared. Disillusionment set in the party. At the end, the court declared him ineligible, and the Congress was re-set for April. The candidates were the incumbent—Adu Boahen, Safo Adu, Dsane Selby, Jones Ofori Atta, J.A. Kufuor and J.H. Mensah. Ofori Atta, who had nominated Adu Boahen in 1992, thought it was time for him to take a bite. J.H. Mensah, the oldest of them all, was the brother-in-law of Kufuor, and there were interesting and embarrassing moments, when the brother-in-law had to publicly abuse his sister's husband.

By this time too, Kufuor had been drained of much interest and some say money. His supporters, who believed he had over-worked, were however confident of his winning. Not an excellent public speaker and lacking charisma to a great degree, Kufuor was however, the best of them all, in terms of one-on-one campaign. He had toured all the constituencies in the country and spoken to the chiefs and more importantly the members of the electoral college who at that time, would decide the fate of the aspirants.

In many places, he was welcome. In other places, the people had made up their minds and would not listen to him.

In the Ejisu-Juaben and Effiduase areas, strong Adu Boahen strongholds, the members of the electoral college did not want to see Kufuor, let alone listen to him. He had the patience to tolerate their contempt for him and in one instance, had to wait for over two hours, to get reluctant party people to listen to him. Kufuor told them it did not matter and that, they should still listen to him with their made-up minds. At Effiduase, a leading Pro-Adu Boahen woman — Mrs. Grace Coleman — even closed the party office, so Kufuor could not get access to her or the other party members. Some of them thought Kufuor was opportunistic, and did not know what the party would gain from a change in leadership since Adu Boahen was better known after contesting the 1992 elections, and should therefore be allowed to use the period to consolidate his position and popularity for the 1996 election.

Apart from about five people who were well educated, Kufuor's campaign team had a grassroots composition. Sometimes, he spent a whole month in a region working on the constituencies such that, seven weeks to the Congress, some of the Adu Boahen strongholds were falling for him. But because these encounters were on a one-on-one basis, and hardly reported in the media, many did not know.

On the other hand, the popularity of Adu Boahen was still rousing. When he spoke on the same platform with Kufuor in Abbey Park, Kumasi, Nkrumah Circle in Accra and most of the major cities, towns and suburbs, it was clear who was the people's choice. He had popular sentiment on his side, and the thousands and thousands of people who cheered him up expected that their representatives, the electoral college, would translate that into voting for him.

The media were not Kufuor friendly, but he had said to friends that "the intimidation of the media is not a bother" since he had done his work well and was sure of victory. He had also told friends that if he should lose the primaries to Adu Boahen for the second time, he would call it quits in politics.

If in 1992 he was not so sure, not this time. For a man who since his days at Prempeh College had seen himself as future president, and even built his huge Accra Airport Residential House in the manner of a presidential palace, perhaps knew what he was about.

On the congress day he left the house late. Many of the delegates who had been hostile during the tour were in his house in the morning to pledge their votes. It delayed his almost triumphant entry to the campus of the University of Ghana. When Kufuor got to the School of Administration, the other aspirants were all seated on the dais. The ovation at his arrival far exceeded the experience in 1992.

Kofi Adusei, who contested for the Party's seat in Bekwai and lost in 1992, but won subsequently in the year 2000, worked as a member of the Kufuor campaign team. He too felt the new energy and told me this.

Though it was always difficult to judge by ovation and cheers leaders command, Kufuor spoke with extraordinary confidence. This time, Haruna Esseku who was one time Central Region Chairman of the NPP nominated him. Alhaji Inusah supported him. Inusah, like Kufuor, had been in the party since the 1960s. A land economist who graduated from the Kwame Nkrumah University of Science and Technology, he was one of the pillars of the Kufuor campaign and the main advisor.

Voting ended at almost midnight. As the votes were being counted, depression, uncertainty and anxiety were visible on the faces of the eight candidates and their wives. There were occasional false conversations among them, but the countenance was one of piety, like school children about to know their examination results.

As the counting got into 2 hours, Kufuor's supporters in the counting room would come to the hall and signal him of good showing in the midst of the brass band music playing all night. As such signals continued and the supporters were unable to hold their excitement, it was becoming clear to Kufuor that he was leading. This was to the discomfort of the other candidates. When they waved to him on the dais, he would do the same; when they smiled, he did the same.

At 1 pm, Sunday morning, when the National Electoral Commission officer announced the final results, the delegates, by their votes, dropped Professor Albert Adu Boahen and gave his mantle to John Agyekum Kufuor. And the mandate was emphatic—Kufuor had collected 1034 of the total votes representing 52% with the Professor trailing with 710 votes representing 35.7%, followed by John Henry Mensah, 110 votes representing 5.5%, Dr.

Jones Ofori Atta with 69 votes representing 3.5%, Kwame Safo Adu, with 42 votes representing 2.1% and Dr. Kofi Dsane Selby, with 24 votes representing 1.2%. The atmosphere was charged beyond belief. After a while, the losers pledged their support to the new leader. Adu Boahen, almost dazed after the announcement, managed to congratulate Kufuor, but not forgetting to add, "I am shocked at the turn of events."

With an excited wife, Theresa, beside him, Kufuor had prepared his victory speech for the long awaited hour and thanked the singing, inattentive delegates, some of whom had started a long march to his Airport Residential Area house in the wee hours of the morning. He said later:

> I knew the end will be good because I took pains to travel up and down the country to measure the mood.

On Sunday evening, Prof. Adu Boahen went to Kufuor's house to formally congratulate him. But the week after was one of uncertainty. The results had upset some Adu Boahen supporters in some parts of the country. The delegates had responded that they knew what they were doing, and that popularity alone, was not a factor with which to elect a presidential candidate.

In the Asante Region, a staunch Adu Boahen supporter, Dr. Kwame Donkor Fordwor, threatened resignation. But all these subsided and vanished when Kufuor began his thanksgiving tour of the country, which was also the beginning of the campaign of the main Opposition leader.

The tour started in Asante, his home base, and the rousing welcome was moving for him. Those who had threatened not to vote in the general elections, were seen in the jubilant crowd. The argument turned this way—"If Kufuor had been able to defeat Adu Boahen, who even in defeat was still popular, then he was the one to watch, the one to beat Rawlings."

After his thanksgiving tour, Kufuor visited the United Kingdom and United States. His external support base had been in these two countries. They had supported him financially. In London, Kufuor addressed supporters of the NPP at a big rally in Seven Sisters, about the conditions in the country. He also spoke to them about strategies to win the upcoming elections. A fund-raising yielded 10,000 pounds sterling for the Party.

A branch of the New Patriotic Party, had been founded in the United States immediately the Danquah-Busia Club was transformed into a party in 1991. Messrs Lawrence Akwasi Agyeman Prempeh and Mohammed Iddris, are credited with the founding, which like the home politics had its Pro-Adu Boahen and Pro-Kufuor supporters. The meetings were in Silver Spring, Maryland. Kufuor had been smart enough to cultivate a base and Akwasi Agyeman Prempeh and Mohammed Iddris became his linkmen. Through them, Kufuor cemented his ties with opinion leaders back in Northern Ghana. Messrs A.B.A. Fuseni, a middle-aged opinion leader, 'COB', and Mustapha Iddris became staunch Kufuor supporters. Later however, Fuseni decided to join the NDC, and there were talks of Kufuor choosing Mustapha Iddris, as his running mate.

Kufuor had himself visited the United States in 1991 to attend the Congressional Breakfast meeting. His good friend at the time was the United States Ambassador to Ghana who extended him the invitation. It was meant for Kufuor to meet influential American politicians. Prempeh and Iddris had also used whatever connections they had for Kufuor to travel around a bit, including a visit to the United States State Department. Even though there was not much to be given in terms of money, psychologically, Kufuor was seen as the one who had all the connections in the United States, and whose frequent travels there, were seen as positive.

With seven months to the national election, Kufuor found himself in limbo. The NPP had to form an alliance with the Nkrumahists and other Opposition Parties if, as some believed, Rawlings were to be defeated in the December election. This delayed his selection of a running mate.

The concept of alliance had been practised by the NDC in the 1992 election, with the EGLE Party founded by Owuraku Amofa, a royal of Akyem Abuakwa, (who broke tradition by joining a party other than one founded by his liberal democrat ancestors), and the National Convention Party, a party made up of some Nkrumahists, who preferred an alliance with the NDC, to the NPP. The Progressive Alliance was the name adopted. Rawlings' running mate and eventual Vice President was Mr. Nkensen Arkaah, the first Ghanaian to obtain an MBA from Harvard Business School and former Chief Executive of major international companies. Mr. Arkaah was in his mid-sixties, and was thus far older than the 48-year-old Rawlings. Nana Konadu Agyeman Rawlings, the President's wife, had served as a Maid of Honor at Arkaah's wedding, and so there was an inter-generational partnership, and "deep misunderstanding that proved unhealthy."

Two years into his position as Vice President to Rawlings, it was clear they were not getting along. Rawlings had shown total public contempt for Arkaah and sidelined him in the activities of Government. The most embarrassing episode was when Arkaah got beaten up by Rawlings at a cabinet meeting held on December 28, 1995, which became a major international disgrace.

Arkaah was becoming more of an opposition figure in

a Government of which he was the Vice President. Whilst many people hated Rawlings, they also questioned how Arkaah, who had shown publicly, his dislike for the Government, could continue to function. What was left to do, many thought, was his resignation.

When the NPP formed its alliance with the Nkrumahists and called it, The Great Alliance (a few months before the 1996 election), Arkaah became the running mate to Kufuor after long negotiations. He became perhaps, the only Vice President in the world, who had to cross-carpet to become a running mate of an Opposition to his previous Government. He became totally controversial. Arkaah's pronouncements, when he was NDC Vice-President, were used by the Government to undermine the Opposition campaign and destroyed whatever good the NPP symbolized. In fact, the NDC needed nothing but to replay the TV footage and radio commentaries of Arkaah, to confirm his double standards. Unfortunately for him too, *The Free Press* came out with a scandalous publication of his affair with a teenage girl—Jemimah Yalley (young enough to be his granddaughter). This was also to hurt the public conscience for a long time and hurt his status as a wonder man.

The Alliance itself never reached firm conclusions on many issues including modalities for selecting parliamentary candidates and in some constituencies, like Ayawaso Central and Korley Klottey in Accra, the parties in the Alliance selected their own candidates, thus splitting the votes and making victory for the NDC.

The Alliance could not also resolve the long-standing ideological issue between the Nkrumahists and Busiaists.

Added to this, the Alliance had little money with which to fight an election in which the incumbent Government was not only well-organized and financially endowed with state resources, but also with virtually all businessmen supporting it.

December 1996 became history, a history of the opposition parties led by John Agyekum Kufuor losing once again to the incumbent President Rawlings. Was Ghana becoming a one party State? Many people asked. Even though the election results of 1996 were slightly better than that of 1992, it raised little hope for the future. Kufuor obtained 40% of the total votes and Rawlings, 58%.

Kufuor accepted the results without many disagreements and attended the inauguration of Jerry John Rawlings as the second President of the Fourth Republic of Ghana. He also attended the parliamentary ceremony in which the elected MPs, of which 66 were from the NPP, were sworn into office. Unlike 1992, the Opposition had little or no excuse to boycott the Parliamentary election as they were held the same day.

Whether Kufuor was capable of becoming the President of Ghana ever, nobody but him and his God knew. What was clear was that, immediately after the swearing-in, he visited a large section of the Ghanaian media, private and State-owned, to thank them for supporting an election in which he lost. Kabral Blay Amihere, the publisher of *The Independent* recalled:

> Against my insistence that he did not need to make an appearance at our offices, and an additional information that I will not be there myself to welcome him, Mr. Kufuor did pay a thank you visit to *The Independent* where he met with my editor Richmond Keelson and the junior staff. That was vintage Kufuor, his ability to touch base with the high and low.

Whether that vintage ability to touch the high and low would see him through the coming years was left to time to tell. In 1998, when U.S. President Bill Clinton visited Ghana, Kufuor was invited to some of the state festivities. After he was introduced to some of the visiting delegates, he jokingly or perhaps sure of his destiny, told them that the next time they come to Ghana, they would meet him as the President of the Republic. This attracted some criticism.

Again, time was to tell.

CHAPTER SEVEN

The Agama Lizard Walks Slowly But It Will Get to Its Destination

Will your anchor hold in the storms of life?
When the clouds unfold their wings of strife?
When the strong tides lift and the cable strain,
Will your anchor drift, or firm remain?

—Priscilla Jane Owens.

The second swearing-in ceremony of Jerry John Rawlings as President on January 7, 1997, saw a new era in the political history of Ghana. It was the first time that an elected Government had completed a term in office, and began the second. Certainly, Jerry John Rawlings, who had that honour was set to be, for now, the longest serving Head of State of Ghana, beating Kwame Nkrumah to that position.

The sixty-six NPP Members of Parliament were equally poised to take their seats. Through an internal arrangement, largely influenced by Kufuor, J.H. Mensah, the oldest of all the MPs, was made the leader of the Opposition. His experience was enormous enough to lead some of the novices to play alternative Government roles. Though the number was insignificant to derail any policies of the NDC or challenge them in any way, many people thought at least, they were capable of serious debate.

By that arrangement, Kufuor also became redundant. He had no role to play within his own party because of the nature of the party's Constitution and also because of the presidential system of Government. He took to attending funerals of party faithfuls and tried as much as possible, to keep hold on the electoral college.

Apart from being recognized internationally as the leader of the Opposition and attendimg conferences abroad, the biggest one hosted by the Commonwealth in February in Kasane, Botswana, on the subject of Democracy and Good Governance, he was waiting impatiently for the party's congress. Having realized how Adu Boahen got involved in so many controversial situations, which cost him the elections, Kufuor stayed clear of issues and became neutral on many. This meant that he could not take serious decisions affecting the party on the same issues.

Still, there were little wars he had to fight. The relationship between him and Peter Ala Adjetey was never good. Whilst Kufuor and his supporters accused Ala Adjetey of sabotaging Kufuor's interest because of his pro-Adu Boahen love, Ala Adjetey's supporters replied that Kufuor lacked the courage to take on important decisions, and thereby, retarded progress.

A coup d' etat, a secret mobilization of a vote of no confidence — allegedly master-minded by Adjetey and other leading members of the party, was exposed. Before this, Ala Adjetey had given scathing remarks about Kufuor's perceived incompetence to *The Daily Graphic.* Kufuor was on a fund-raising tour in the United States and had to rush back home to defend himself — a defence which started when Kwadwo Mpiani, (one of Kufuor's personal assistants), in an equally angry tone in the same *Daily Graphic,* cast aspersions against the Chairman.

The stage, many thought, was being set for another confusion and leadership crisis in the party.

Meanwhile, the sixty-six NPP MPs were mounting pressure on the ruling NDC Government with J.H. Mensah, Nana Akuffo Addo, Dr. Kofi Konadu Apraku, Malik Al-Hassan Yakubu, Osafo Marfo, Dr. Kwame Addo Kufuor and others, emerging as leading lights and possible challengers to Kufuor.

But Kufuor was still controlling the electoral college, having given them no cause to think otherwise. He was popular and capable of using the college to change some of the executives who were against him.

It did not take very long for August 1998 to come, when the NPP had its Congress to elect new executives. Realizing that the signals were not good and that he could possibly lose, Peter Ala Adjetey decided not to contest the Chairmanship position again.

The Party had lost two major elections and there was a general feeling of bringing in more young people into the executive. Again, the voter statistics in Ghana released by

93

the National Electoral Commission, showed that over 70 percent of registered voters were between the ages of 18 and 39, and therefore the need to appeal to the youth was strong. Among the candidates to emerge this time for executive positions and who eventually won, were Odoi Skyes, 62, a lawyer who had been with the tradition for many years and previously served as an MP and a diplomat and Dan Botwe, then 39, who had worked in the Party as Director of Operations and Research since 1996 and had travelled extensively in the country. He defeated the long serving Secretary and weary, old Agyenim Boateng. Kwesi Brew, a well-known poet, became Treasurer, replacing Hackman Owusu Agyeman. Ama Busia became First Vice, Wayo Senin became Second Vice and Dr. Kwaku Afriyie, Third Vice.

As is typical, the new executive was reflective of which presidential candidate was popular. Its profile was favourable to Kufuor, for almost all of them had had his good-will even though Dan Botwe thought that was not necessarily the case.

> I was expecting to win. I was confident of winning.
> I did not factor that into my campaign but you
> cannot also rule it out that the electorate who will
> be voting will consider that.

The NPP, quite interestingly had by this time, amended the party's Constitution such that a presidential candidate, should be chosen two years before national elections. This was something that favoured Kufuor, and which his strategists, had worked out. Believing that a day is a long time in politics, they made sure that, whilst Kufuor was popular, he got elected. This was an argument, which the Adu Boahen strategists had used, but didn't work.

By this time, it was clear that J.H. Mensah, without

doubt the leading Opposition figure and MP for Sunyani-West as well as Nana Akuffo Addo MP for Akyem Abuakwa and Shadow Attorney-General, Dr. Kofi Kondua Apraku, MP for Offinso South and Minority Spokesman on Finance, Alhaji Malik Al-Hassan Yakubu, Shadow Minister of Interior, Kwame Kodua, a lawyer, were keen to contest Kufuor.

These people, like the others, had resisted an early Congress and thought it was a carefully planned strategy for Kufuor to secure the mandate, but not much could be done since by the party's amended Constitution, October 28, 1998 had been fixed for the Congress.

Of all the candidates the two that posed the greatest challenge to Kufuor were Nana Akuffo Addo and J.H. Mensah.

Nana Akuffo Addo, turned 53 in 1998. His father, Edward Akuffo Addo, was once Chief Justice of Ghana and later President (1969-72). Nana Addo, had apart from an impressive father's achievements that started at Oxford University, campaigned against military dictatorship and human rights abuse in Ghana since he was in his late 20s, and served as the General-Secretary of the People's Movement for Freedom and Justice, in 1978. He was instrumental in setting up the Ghana Commission on Human Rights. Educated at Lancing College, Sussex, England, he was at Oxford briefly and continued at the University of Ghana where he studied for a B.S.c in Economics. Nana Addo was called to the English Bar (Middle Temple) in July 1971, and the Ghanaian Bar in July, 1975. He was an Associate Counsel of Coudert Freres (Brothers), a major U.S. Law Firm, at its Paris Office in France and junior member of the Chambers, U.V. Campbell. He was also a Senior Partner and Co-founder with Dr. Edmund Prempeh of the prominent law firm, Akuffo-Addo, Prempeh and Co. in 1979. He was a Member/Fellow of many professional associations in and outside of Ghana.

J.H. Mensah (72), on the other hand, started work as Assistant Inspector of Taxes of the Government of Ghana in 1953—that is—four years before Ghana became independent, and when J.A. Kufuor, was a teenager. He later worked as a Research Fellow and lecturer in Economics at the University College of the Gold Coast till 1958. He moved to New York to work for the United Nations as an Economic Affairs Officer, Center for Development Planning, Projections and Policies. He returned to Ghana again to become the Executive Secretary of the National Planning Commission, Government of Ghana, and moved on to become the Minister of Finance in the Busia Government of 1969-72. J.H. Mensah also served in many international advisory roles including negotiations of ECOWAS in Somalia, Ghana, and Liberia and also re-negotiated the East-African Common Market Treaty between 1965-66.

Of the three, Dr. Apraku had the less experience in politics. A Professor in Economics, he was Head of the Economic Reconstruction and Co-ordination Unit of the United Nations in Croatia, formerly Republic of Yugoslavia from 1995-1996. Before that, he was an Economics Professor at the University of North Carolina between 1987-1995. His previous appointments included teaching at the Wheeling University, West Virginia, and team Leader of the United Nations Mission to South Africa for its General Elections in May 1994. He returned to Ghana through the encouragement of Prof. Adu Boahen, to serve as his Economic Advisor when he, Adu Boahen, was leading the Opposition movement. But, he also worked briefly as Head of Policy Planning and Analysis of the Ministry of Agriculture. His Ph.D specialization was in Agricultural Economics, an interest cultivated when he was a little boy growing tomatoes at his little village in

Akumadan in the Asante Region. He represented that Constituency in Parliament.

What however impressed most Ghanaians was the professionalism with which Nana Addo handled his challenge to Kufuor. There was enough money for him to acquire about ten cars for campaigning all over the country. When his formal declaration was made, it became a big media event with some FM Stations broadcasting it live. There were more then three fax machines operating in his campaign headquarters and uncountable mobile phones that connected him and the team to everywhere he went.

Because of his long involvement in the struggle against dictatorship and especially his leadership of the Alliance for Change, he had befriended many journalists and publishers and had had the foresight to establish his own private newspaper — *The Statesman*, which is one of the well-circulated newspapers in the country. This was seven years before this day of challenge. All the top-flight publications and low circulating ones — *The Ghanaian Chronicle, The Statesman, The Dispatch, The Guide, The Weekly Insight* were for Nana Addo. They had paid for advertisements for him and they volunteered free ones as well. It was only *The Independent* that came out publicly to root for Kufuor.

Once the media had focused on these two, they made the others irrelevant and it was either because they were truly irrelevant, or the media pushed them there.

Whilst Nana Akuffo Addo proved that he could mobilize the resources to lead the party to victory should he be voted for, there were others who saw him as a snob and too high class conscious. The only media blemish in his campaign was when he confronted the publisher of *The Independent*, Kabral Blay Amihere for using a bad picture of him; an issue, which attracted the headline —*Akuffo Addo, Attacks The Independent.* According to Kabral:

Whilst *The Independent* might have given indica-
tions that it supported Kufuor, we had not decided
to use our paper to destroy any candidate and had
indeed given the Akuffo Addo campaign favourable
coverage in our paper

The Ghanaian Chronicle had predicted in the days to
the election that 'Nana Akuffo Addo would win hands
down. The paper "did not think Kufuor was articulate
enough neither did he have grasp of the issues." There
were published surveys in which editors of the private
media including Kwesi Pratt, Kwesi Biney and Kwaku
Baako, all predicted a Nana Addo victory.

As this urban politics was going on, Kufuor had become
a scarce commodity, deep down in the forest country,
savanna belt and other non-urban areas. His only fax
machine in his house was difficult to get through. Without
the resources to buy cars and mobile phones, he was deeply
with the electoral college members. He said in an interview
later with me in London in December of 1998:

I was not bothered in the least with media criticisms that even attempted to question my intellectual capacity and doubted whether I even went to
Oxford.

The Independent, very sure of a Kufuor victory, had
come out with a special issue on October 22, titled NPP,
GO FOR KUFUOR. According to the Publisher, their
own survey after travelling to all the regional capitals and
to the villages, showed a Kufuor victory. Of the two thousand votes, the paper predicted that Kufuor would collect
one thousand three hundred, Nana Addo, five hundred,
and the other candidates—J. H. Mensah, Alhaji Malik
Al-Hassan Yakubu, John Kwame Kodua and Dr. Kofi

Apraku, splitting the remaining two hundred.

The contest brought its own family tension. To campaign against his brother-in-law, J.H. Mensah had to be diplomatic, but how could he be diplomatic against an opponent in a presidential contest? To cool matters, Dr. Amoako Tuffuor had gone to Mrs. Theresa Kufuor to impress on her, the need to advise J.H. Mensah to stand down. Tuffuor's investigations had proved Kufuor would win. Mrs. Kufuor who was embarrassed about the whole situation, had spent months in London possibly avoiding this, and told Tuffour it would be difficult for her to do that "since everybody was fighting for his head."

The party Congress was held at Sunyani in the Brong Ahafo region. After the general state of the party address, the aspirants got introduced again. J.H. Mensah spoke contemptuously, telling the delegates to reject Mr. Kufuor, like an expired Cassava. He told the delegates that Kufuor had become useless, a declaration, which was met with boos and cat-calls such that, his whole rendition for the evening was incoherent.

Again, it was deep into the night before the voting ended and the results declared.

John Agyekum Kufuor made history again with an overwhelming majority of the votes—One thousand two hundred and eight-six (1286), fourteen votes less than *The Independent* predicted and representing 64.8%. Nana Addo got Six hundred and twenty-six (628) votes, one hundred and twenty-eight more than *The Independent* predicted and representing 31.6%. Dr. Kofi Konadu Apraku had Fifty-two (52) representing 2.6%. John Kwame Kodua, eight (8) votes representing 0.445%, Malik Al-Hassan Yakubu, Seven (7) votes representing 0.35% and J.H. Mensah, three (3) votes representing 0.15%.

In his speech after the declaration of results, Nana Addo, said:

Today, the battle has ended; the people have spoken. I whole-heartedly accept the outcome of today's election and I wish, in the tradition of our great party, to congratulate Mr. J. A. Kufuor for his decisive and striking first round-victory today. Now, we have a leader in Kufuor. I pledge my confidence and support for him in our quest to wrestle power from the NDC in Election 2000. We must put our shoulders to the wheel and work relentlessly until the NPP forms the next Government on January 7, 2001. I've seen it written. In future we'll see what happens. For now, we'll make sure we work to ensure that in the year 2001, Mr. Agyekum Kufuor is sworn in as the next President of Ghana.

A happy J.A. Kufuor gave his victory speech, a joyous wife by his side. J.H. Mensah had quickly reverted to a position of a brother-in-law and stood by Kufuor's side. Kufuor said:

Mr. Chairman, Your Excellencies, National Executive Officers of our Great Party, Honorable Members of Parliament, Distinguished Guests and delegates, early this morning, I made a passionate appeal to you for a renewal of the trust you reposed in me for the1996 elections.

This time around, it is to enable me to attempt the 2000 elections as the flag-bearer of our great party. I must confess how overwhelmed I am of your massive endorsement of my person and candidature for the next elections.

My first message to our political opponents is simply this: the NPP now has its flag-bearer in the

100

person of John Agyekum Kufuor for the 2000 election and this means business.

I wish to thank delegates for giving me a rare and unprecedented second term. I pledge to leave no stone unturned and spare no effort to lead the party to prepare itself thoroughly in all departments in terms of securing logistics, party cohesion and organization.

We will start by penetrating all the 10 regions of the country for resounding victory in the year 2000.

I count on the total co-operation and support of all friends at home and abroad and also from former aspirants.

The gentlemen who lost today to me have talents and proven abilities the party and Ghana need. I invite them to join hands with me so that together we can break the jinx of our party being in perpetual opposition.

Once again, I extend my gratitude to you all especially the National Executive for organizing a successful congress.

To my office staff and members of my network throughout the length and breadth of Ghana, I will eternally be indebted to you for this honour. To the press, I also extend my gratitude for the publicity you gave me throughout my campaigns. To the anonymous sponsors of my cause, I pray God will abundantly reward you for supporting a just cause. Without you, the going would have been very, very tough indeed. To Ghanaians, especially the ordinary man on the street that cheered me on, I promise not to let you down. I will continue to need your support in the years ahead.

To the NPP branches in the United States,

United Kingdom, Canada and elsewhere who supported me, accept my sincerest gratitude. I will
need your help in the years ahead.

Finally, I want to thank my devoted wife whose
support and sacrifices have been immeasurable.

Mr. Chairman, it is with great humility and
honour that I acknowledge the delegates' massive
endorsement of me as a flag-bearer of our dear
party for Election 2000. Together, we will work
hard, very hard, to ensure victory in 2000.

May God and Allah send you home safely and
continue to bless you all in the years ahead.

Thank you.

CHAPTER EIGHT

A Long Journey Ends at Sunrise

Many that we loved have left us, reaching first their journey's end; now they wait to give us welcome, brother, sister, child and friend; when at last our journey is over and we pass away from sight, Father, take us through the darkness into everlasting light.

—The Hymnist.

In return for all these services, I ask for no monument of praise, no sign of honour, save an eternal remembrance of this day.

—Cicero.

B y being elected for the second time as the Presidential Candidate of the New Patriotic Party, Kufuor had made history. For a party which prides itself as having the best intellectuals in the country and in which many people want to be president, some simply because they have high academic credentials, and others, because they are real achievers, trust in leadership is always in short supply. But Kufuor, by the election, had two years to campaign, enough time to make an impact on his previous showing.

The Party tradition also had a handicap, for having been in opposition for over twenty years without any strong sources of raising money, the burden of raising campaign money, rested on the presidential candidate. Drained of all resources himself by 1999, not much campaign was seen. The Party's vehicles were virtually broken. It did not have a single car in the nine regions outside Accra, and the two cars in Accra, were in bad condition. The party's telephone bills were unpaid for months and in the regional and district capitals all over Ghana, lease agreements with landlords for office space, were not fulfilled. Then, the controversy of who would pay for cars credited to the NPP for the 1996 elections, emerged. Whilst the car company, Concordia, wrote to the party demanding payment of 100,000 dollars, Party Chairman Peter Ala Adjetey argued that, technically, the party did not enter into any agreement with the company and therefore could not be held responsible. Presidential candidate Kufuor, he said, was the one who signed the agreement for his presidential campaign. The party also owed Auto Parts Company of Ghana, about the same amount.

For a party that intended to assume power, these were bad signals. Securing campaign money, thus rested on the presidential candidate. If the candidate was financially incapable to run the campaign, he commanded little respect and if financially endowed, he could have his way with the party's image and apparatus. People also questioned the sincerity of some of the losers in the previous party primaries, when they expressed difficulty in helping finance the campaign. Particularly, Nana Akuffo Addo who, whilst campaigning for the presidential candidate slot, could afford over ten cars, but looked the other way, when his party was in dire need.

The early election of Kufuor, while necessary to reduce inner conflict for the candidate, the campaign did not take the advantage to develop strategies. His critics intensified their campaign against him and argued about how Akuffo Addo would have been a better choice. The duty of a leader is the ability to mobilize resources and if Kufuor could not do that, then, he was simply incompetent, the arguments went. The Party Secretariat itself was disillusioned. The General-Secretary, Dan Botwe, a young man with a wife and children to feed, was doing his job on a voluntary basis. The Chairman, Odoi Skyes, according to close party sources, wanted , to resign. Virtually everybody from Kufuor to the messenger at the Secretariat, was a volunteer.

Kufuor's numerous travels to the United States and United Kingdom did not bring much money and he himself looked desperate.

Interestingly, it was Prof. Fred Sai, a distinguished AIDS Consultant to the United Nations and currently President of the Ghana Academy of Arts and Sciences, who at this critical time, donated ten pick-ups for the party to start its campaign. Prof. Sai had campaigned to be the Chairman of the NPP but was not supported by the Kufuor delegates since he was pro-Adu Boahen, but he still gave; a situation that Kufuor fans used against Akuffo Addo for his lack of interest in Kufuor's campaign.

It was in such a trying moment that Dr. Jones Ofori

Atta threw a "bomb" at a desperate party. A press release announced his resignation from politics. That itself was not as disturbing as the implication it had for Kufuor's leadership. The release was the lead story in the state con-trolled *Daily Graphic,* and it was highly politicized. Whilst many Party supporters thought the timing was very bad, it was perfect though, for the NDC. It showed the lack of confidence by the distinguished Economist, in Kufuor's leadership, and they made it seem so.

When later, Kwame Pianim, another distinguished Economist who had been the NPP spokesman on Eco-nomics and Finance resigned from the party with huge publicity, it was not only alarming, but also devastating. Pianim, like Ofori Atta, saw himself as perhaps, more qualified to lead the party than anybody else. His reasons for resignation, were to enable him reconcile the political parties in the country, and form a national government. That is to say, he saw himself as working towards political resolution, in the aftermath of the election. Again, the NDC played on this and equated it to lack of confidence in Kufuor.

Vincent Assiseh, the Party's Press-Secretary, in a radio interview in Accra even said that the NDC would most welcome Pianim and put him in a position in their party, where his services to the nation would be most effective. The NPP, he said, could never win power.

Apart from these high level resignations, what became known as 'Defects', assumed notoriety in the country's politics. It was a situation where members, most often of the NPP, were alleged to have resigned to join the NDC. They would pose in front of TV and still cameras and attract huge publicity. They said uncomplimentary things about the Party and its "confused and insincere leadership and hoped the NDC was the only party to save Ghana."

The NPP would sometimes deny these, and they

argued that the so-called defectors were not known even in their constituencies and were only a "shameless rented crowd".

One defection that really damaged Kufuor but which perhaps also won him sympathy, was that of his own confidential Campaign Manager, Alhaji Inusah. For someone who had been with the NPP tradition for almost forty years, it was big news. Interestingly, Alhaji chose no other time than when Kufuor had left the country. He had planned this with leading members of the NDC and so when Kufuor had a hint of this in London, he immediately phoned Alhaji Inusah and for over two hours, convinced him not to do that in his absence but to no avail.

The Alhaji had already arranged with the NDC Youth Organizer, E.T. Mensah, and the Press-Secretary Vincent Assiseh, to have a press conference to announce the resignation that day. Indeed, immediately after his conversation with Kufuor, he went to the NDC party office and denounced him.

Luckily for the NPP, the NDC Government was itself afflicted with problems. Earlier in 2000, it had become clear that the NDC would need somebody to succeed Rawlings who, after two terms, could not contest elections again. To prevent what some said was his wife, Nana Konadu Agyeman Rawlings' ambition to also become president the husband nominated his Vice, Prof. Atta Mills, and urged all NDC supporters to vote for him . This became known as "The Swedru Declaration" (the support for Prof. Mills having been declared at Swedru). The implications were that the NDC would not have a Congress for the delegates to choose whom they thought fit, and even so, who would stand for parliamentary election. To many people in the NDC itself, this was undemocratic since the party had since its formation never selected its own leaders. People like Alhaji Mahama

Iddrisu, who had served in the Rawlings military Government and continued in the NDC, were clearly frustrated, but could not quit.

Goosie Tandoh, a 48-year-old lawyer trained at the University of Ghana Law School and at Northwestern University in the United States, emerged as a rebel against what he described as lack of internal politics in the NDC. Having worked as a close associate of Rawlings and his friend, Tsatsu Tsikata, at the Ghana National Petroleum Corporation (GNPC), Tandoh decided to form a new party out of the NDC, which he called The National Reform Party. It had people like Osei Kyeretwie, who also worked at GNPC, as General-Secretary. The Reform Party was supported strongly by the private media, which stressed the issue of inner conflict within the NDC. For the first time, there were cracks, and more significantly, these occurred at a time that Rawlings could not stand for elections again.

Owuraku Amofa, founder of the EGLE Party and Deputy Minister of Tourism, also left the party frustrated, and against the one-man declaration of support for Mills. That also meant that the NDC's alliance that helped them win the 1996 election, was coming apart.

Around this same time, world prices for Ghana's commodities fell. The price of gold had gone from bad to worse and Ashanti Goldfields and its Chief Executive, Sam Jonah, had come under uncalled for attacks, from Rawlings. Jonah had engaged in the complex investment opportunity of hedging in oil, which added to the misfortunes of AGC's shares on the New York Stock Exchange and other listed ones in Europe. The price of Cocoa had also gone down. This meant that export revenue had decreased, and the Government could not fulfill some of its development initiatives and obligations, such as servicing its debts. There was also the problem of the State finance for the coming election, with the currency that had experienced over 40 percent depreciation. Because of the internal frustrations that had set in for the NDC as well as leakages of damaging information from within, the party for the first time looked   fragile. Corruption charges ran rampant. For between 1992 and 1999, the media,   especially the private print led by *The Ghanaian Chronicle*, had exposed corruption on an unprecedented level. Over 120 cases of local and high level international syndicated crimes committed by members of Government, were exposed. The media dared some individuals to challenge their allegations, which included Ministers sending their children to American universities, whilst the local educational system rotted. There were allegations of government officials holding bank accounts in Britain, Europe and America. Rawlings himself had become a victim, for, at a time when many children could not pass the basic level examination due to lack of text books and other materials, he had sent his first daughter to study at Dublin University. J. H. Owusu Acheampong, his Majority Leader, had sent his three children to American universities and, supposedly, was paying over 75,000 dollars a year, whilst he received a monthly salary of less then 500 dollars!

As the exposures got huge media publicity in a country with a critical and independent print media and over 45 FM radios in all regions but the Upper-East, many heard of what was going on. The virtual silent response of the Government, was interpreted as an admission of guilt, which made things worse for their image. This angered people and they openly spoke out, asking the Government to either deny or confirm the stories.

Rawlings, had in 1979, executed three former Heads-of-State and senior army officers on corruption charges that included some who legitimately borrowed money from banks. He handed over power to the elected Government of the late Dr. Hilla Limann, only to stage another coup, because the Government was accused of corruption. Now, Ghanaians were reading and hearing of serious corruption allegations for which the Government had no answers.

What also became a factor in the upcoming election was the NDC Government's Foreign Affairs policy. Since adopting the Structural Adjustment Programme of the World Bank and the IMF in 1982, Rawlings' attitude to the West changed to be friendlier. They reciprocated by pampering the regime. It enabled Rawlings to pay an official visit to America and to meet with President Bill Clinton; it enabled him to visit Britain to meet Prime Minister Tony Blair and even addressed the Scottish Parliament. The Scottish were not that friendly as they taunted him for not knowing his Scottish father. The Queen of England, Elizabeth II, also visited Ghana and later Bill Clinton also visited.

Ekow Spio Garbrah who had been appointed Ambassador to the United States in 1992, is credited with working out some of these graceful public relations works. A smart young man educated in the United States, he worked for the Public Affairs Department of the Africa Development Bank and later became Minister of Education and Communication. He played a prominent role in the NDC campaign and media strategies.

On the other side, Rawlings rose to become Chairman of the Economic Community of West African States (ECOWAS), and through his appointee, Dr. Mohammed Ibn Chambas, played a significant role in the Liberian Civil War. But despite these positive foreign policy issues, Ghana's relations with her immediate neighbors since 1981, were problematic. Togo especially, but also Burkina Faso, and Ivory Coast previously accused Rawlings of meddling in their internal affairs and encouraging dissidents to stage coups. Some had for long wished for his demise.

The upcoming election was of interest to them since

with a good neighbour one could sleep in peace without thinking too much of security.

It was in such an atmosphere of difficult odds that the NDC had to fight this election. Any opposition leader would be happy with such a situation and Kufuor, indeed, was. For he had many campaign themes against the NDC.

To get set for the election which was less than a year away, Kufuor at the last congress of the NPP in Accra, selected his running mate. It had long been a guessing game but Kufuor had kept the issue close to his chest. Hawa Yakubu, a very ambitious former MP for Bawku-Central, was expected to be nominated. The possibility that Nana Akuffo Addo could also be considered for the position, died quickly, because of the concern that the ticket would have two Akans. The ethnic politics of the nation did not encourage such a team.

At last, it rested on Alhaji Aliu Mahama, who comes from Yendi in Northern Ghana and has Nigerian ancestry on his father's side.

A graduate in Engineering from the Kwame Nkrumah University of Science and Technology, he was an unknown quantity in Ghanaian politics. His selection by Kufuor surprised many. But Alhaji Mahama had money, some said, is a Muslim and hopefully a big attraction for votes, and was one of the behind-the-scenes players who footed some of Kufuor's bills.

His ethnic background helped relax the perception of the NPP as an Akan party. As Aliu himself said in his acceptance speech, by his nomination, the NPP has a "forest boy" (referring to Kufuor's country-side background) and a "Zongo boy"(his own "strangers quarters" or immigrant status part), to ensure the victory of the party.

An NPP campaign Management Team was headed by Jake Obetsebi- Lamptey, an astute Public Relations and Marketing Consultant, and CEO of one of the biggest advertising agencies, Lintas. Obetsebi-Lamptey's father was one of the Big Six, and who together with Kwame Nkrumah, led the anti-colonial struggle and got imprisoned for it. A former friend of Rawlings, he and those in the team, mounted an extensive and very exciting campaign that at first matched the NDC boot for boot and later, passed it. The campaign, choreographed in all the local languages were in drama, comedy, well-packaged rallies shown on TV with a lot of propaganda added to it.

The Young Executive Forum, a wing of NPP business-men, partly bankrolled the campaign.

But two things stood out. The Electoral Commission placement of the NPP at the bottom of the voting card was also adopted by the campaign to their advantage. "Aseho," which means "The Bottom," was an expression used to simply tell illiterate voters that on polling day, they should just thumbprint "Aseho" and the change, the Positive Change of Ghanaian life, which the party had long promised, would start.

If that became a sign of expression, it also became a sign of greeting and the campaign theme symbol. So pop-ular was this invention and dictation of the party that it forced the NDC to also invent "Esroho," meaning "The Top." which in another interesting way told illiterate NDC voters that they should thumb-print the first pic-ture on the ballot paper which was that of Prof. Atta Mills.

And then the song. Never in the history of political campaign has a gospel or religious song played an influen-tial role the way Cindy Thompson's "Messiah" tape did. "Awurade Kasa," a track song on this tape captured the spiritual yearning of the nation. Translated as "Lord Speak," the lyrics are of someone living in a nation in despair, a nation in search of direction but tried, as it could, found none. It runs:

112

Lord speak so my heart will be at rest.

Lord have mercy on me because overwhelming
troubles have made me speechless.

Whatever work I do, I don't succeed.

Worst, the sorrows in my marriage, the sorrows
that surround my whole personality.

Lord, do you see these sorrows?

Do you exist at all?

If you do not speak to me, if you do not bless me, I
will not stop wailing and my heart will bleed till
I die.

Lord speak so my heart will be at rest.

Though Cindy's tape was a political coincidence, sales
rose so high and enriched the singer, with her popularity
rising as well. It became the campaign song and on Ghana
Television, TV 3, radio and in churches, it was a metaphor
for God's blessings and also for a change of government.

As it increased in sales, a group of young ladies from
Tamale also composed Messiah's political equivalent titled
"J.A. Kufuor." The lyrics are also of a people under serious
oppression and suppression with only J.A. Kufuor, a man
of vision and gentility, left to rescue them and make
Ghana a happy home.

Suddenly, a New Patriotic Party that months ago was
so cash-strapped had mobilized enough money to acquire
not only cars, but also motorcycles and bicycles for
campaign in all the regions of the country.

Front-page advertisements in the print media, prime
time allocation on all FM stations in the country and on
the three TV Stations, the State owned Ghana Television,
TV3 and Metro TV, had surprised many people. This
time, it was not only in major towns and cities that one
could see the NPP paraphernalia, but in the villages as
well. It also suddenly increased Kufuor's respectability and

gave him firm leadership over the party.

The NDC, sitting on an economy that was over-heated and with increase in OPEC prices of oil, which necessitated an immediate increase in petroleum prices, but which was politically unwise for the Government to pass on to the consumer, the nation's financial situation worsened.

By July, Kufuor, already on a country tour that would bring him back to Accra in September, had mounted an extensive campaign mainly by damaging the NDC's moral fibre, accusation of local and syndicated international crime connections.

And the NPP campaign cash, suspected by many critics to have come from sources other than Ghana, also became a political issue. Monies were given to all the 200 MPs standing on the party's ticket, to intensify the campaign and even though the NDC would later unofficially accuse the Nigerian Government of General Obasanjo of bankrolling the Opposition in Ghana, it would be hard to prove.

Of course, some NPP members and other Ghanaians (including the NPP MP for Bawku Central, Madam Hawa Yakubu, Joe Baidoo Ansah and Kufuor himself, had a good relationship with the Nigerian leader. But it is Ken Ofori Atta, who established Databank Financial Services in Accra after working as a broker with prestigious brokerages in New York, who is General Obasanjo's best known friend in Ghana before he even became President of Nigeria). The aftermath of the election and the sudden excellent relationship that existed between Ghana, Togo, Senegal, Ivory Coast and Burkina Faso and their Presidents Gnassingbe Eyadema, Abdoulaye Wade, Laurent Gbagbo and Blaise Compaore, had convinced some without proof of the NDC's accusation.

Domestically, local churches all over the country were also caught in the feverish mood for a change. In churches, the innuendoes in prayer form against the Government were telling. On FM radio early morning devotion hour, the preachers especially in Accra and Kumasi, told their congregation to vote for a change of government.

The National Electoral Commission, playing its neutral role was equally mindful of the religious dimension. On November 15, 2000, *The Evening News* reported, "Ghanaians Cry to God for Peaceful Elections." It said, "The Electoral Commission will hold a prayer and fasting session on Friday November 24 at the Conference Hall of the Commission.

This is to seek the driving intervention of God for peace and stability to prevail during the presidential and parliamentary elections in December."

To advance Ghana's democratic base, the Ghana Journalists Association, the Ghana Broadcasting Corporation and the Freedom Forum, an American NGO, for the first time brought together, all the seven presidential candidates for a debate at the Accra International Centre on September 27. The NDC surprisingly backed out of the debate, accusing the selected journalists who were to do the questioning as anti-NDC thus, attracting more media criticisms of fear for their sins and as some believed, to prevent more embarrassing questions on accountability.

The seven, apart from Kufuor and Vice President Atta Mills, were Dr. Edward Mahama, of the People's National Convention, Dr. Charles Wereko Brobby of the United Ghana Movement, Prof. George Hagan of the Convention Peoples Party, Goosie Tandoh of The National Reform Party and Dan Lartey of the Great Consolidated Peoples' Party. The debate, which was later broadcast by the CNN, also caused the NDC some embarrassment for non-participation.

By this time, Kufuor, who had almost lost his voice from continuous non-stop campaign trips, was pulling the crowds wherever he went.

Instead of the NDC putting Prof. Atta Mills at the forefront, Rawlings, who was the out-going President, was the one leading the campaign rallies. Worst, Atta Mills had promised Ghanaians that if he was elected, he would consult Rawlings 24 hours a day, a point that Kufuor and the NPP politicized as Mills lacking independence, and Rawlings ruling by proxy, should Mills win.

Later, realizing the damage the Rawlings leadership of the campaign was having, Atta Mills gave his fantastic "I am in Motion" speech, which sort of explained how he was his own man and how his genuine desire for likely consultation with Rawlings, had been politicized to negative effect.

When December 8, 2000 came, the acrimony, violence and bloodshed that people had anticipated with the elections were absent. That was the third time since 1992, that the national elections had been violence free. Many had acquired some experience. As early as 2 a.m., people had started forming queues in major towns and villages and by 7am when officers of the Electoral Commission reported to the posts, people were ready to start voting.

Kufuor, who had transferred his vote from Atwima to Accra, voted near his Airport Residential area with his wife, Theresa, and daughter Nana Ama. By mid-day, the radio stations were reporting smooth voting patterns. Those who finished voting went to their homes and others sat near the polling station till 5pm to hear the results.

There were great vigils all over the country with party supporters monitoring FM stations for the latest results. By the early hours of December 9, it was becoming clear that the NPP was in the lead in both the presidential and parliamentary elections. At the Ghana International Press Centre in Accra where many journalists were verifying reports, and at the NPP headquarters where a crowd was milling such that it was impossible to enter, an NPP win was becoming evident. Results from NDC strong-holds in Accra showed NPP winning.

In the early hours of December 11, it was clear the NPP had won a parliamentary majority, increased the number of its parliamentary seats from 66 to 99 with the NDC maintaining 92 seats. Four independent candidates also won seats and with the Convention People's Party having a seat and three seats going to the People's National Convention. One seat was undecided. That itself was devastating to the government party.

The Independent newspaper came out on December 11 with a headline, Change, Change; Change at Last, And the Winner is Kufuor. It was said that *The Daily Graphic* had also printed an earlier edition declaring Kufuor the winner but had to destroy it. All these were before Dr. Afari Gyan, the Electoral Commissioner, came out to declare a 'No Winner' in the election. Kufuor was leading with over 300,000 votes and tactically, the winner. Kufuor's 48.44 percent (3,131,739 votes) was however less than the almost 52 percent required by the electoral rules, to grant him an uncontested lead. Prof. Mills of the NDC had 44.8 percent (2,895,675 votes). There was therefore to be run-off elections for the two leading vote earners in the presidential contest.

December 28 was fixed for the presidential re-run between Kufuor and Mills. Meanwhile, CNN was showing Kufuor celebrating his birthday on December 8, and drinking Champagne with thousands of people who had thronged to his Airport Residential Area residence. They included those who had a few days earlier, written him off.

The unsettled results caused some disillusionment. Some within the NPP, were disappointed that despite their impressive showing, they could still not receive enough votes to have the matter rest on the first go.

But with "Kufuor already behaving like a president," as *The Economist* described the atmosphere at his house, it was plain to anybody who knew the politics of run-off in Ghana and Africa, that Kufuor would win again on December 28.

The first round results really upset whatever strategy the NDC had. Though they had admitted the election was going to be difficult, they had hoped to win. Within days, Kufuor had hit the road again but with Atta Mills immobilized by the results, it took the NDC over a week to start campaigning.

The strategy, when they recovered from the stupor, was dirty. The team, headed by Ekow Spio-Garbrah, the Minister of Education, carried adverts in both the state –owned and private electronic media that attacked the personality of Kufuor. But for everything they said, there were a thousand and one responses. Ghanaians, it became clear, had made up their minds and were only waiting for December 28 to come. The other presidential candidates had asked all their supporters to give their votes to Kufuor in the second round. The die was almost cast and on the TV and radio, Cindy Thompson's lyrics dominated again:

> Lord speak so my heart will be at rest!
> Lord have mercy on me because overwhelming
>   troubles have made me speechless.
> Whatever work I do, I don't succeed. Worst, the
>   sorrows in my marriage, the sorrows that sur-
>   round my whole personality.
> Lord, do you see these sorrows? Do you exist at all?
> If you do not speak to me, if you do not bless me, I
>   will not stop wailing and my heart will bleed till
>   I die.
> Lord speak so my heart will be at rest.

On December 28, the voting was massive. Again, at midnight, people kept vigil singing with greater intensity

118

and commitment this time. As the results started coming in, it was clear again that Kufuor had taken an early lead with bigger margins. By mid-day of December 29, it was known all over the country that the hour of change had come. But still, the Constitution mandated the Electoral Commissioner, Dr. Afari Gyan, as the sole person to announce the final results. As people waited for this formality to be done, Dr. Afari Gyan gave an interview on the BBC Focus on Africa Programme on Friday. He told BBC's Robin White that it would be difficult for the NDC to close the over 500,000 votes gap.

In the evening of that Friday at 7.00 pm, Prof. John Atta Mills, did the overdue thing and called the home of J.A. Kufuor, and congratulated him for winning the elections and wished him the best of luck.

In a telephone conversation I had with him in Accra at this victory moment, Kufuor said:

> I should give credit to my associates. They may not be described as mainstream politicians but I tell you, they were thorough in their support. It is unfortunate Alhaji Inusah allowed himself to be overtaken by what I will describe, as "political misfortune."
>
> He allowed himself to be side-tracked when victory was looming. He just could not see it. So he left. But he played a good part. Tommy Amematekpor is more a businessman who declared faith in me from 1991 and he stuck with me through and through. Then there was Gabriel (Gabby) Nketia, another businessman who stayed with me from the 1980s as well as a Special Assistant and friend Kwadwo Mpiani, who was with me in Parliament and an old school mate.

It was in this state of victory that Victor Owusu passed

away in London on December 16, ten days short of his seventy-seventh birthday. He had been informed of Kufuor's first round success before he became comatose. Victor however departed to the ancestors, so the elders including Kufuor believed, with messages of good tidings.

Life has its turn of ironies. And so Victor Owusu's failure, was also his success. For it was not so much a storyline of he who sought the presidency and by twist of fate did not get it, as he who adopted and groomed a protégée to whom fate was kinder, and blessed.

When he was sworn in as President, Kufuor honoured Victor Owusu with a state burial and before the eyes of the nation's TV cameras, wept. As the noble historian and biographer, Ivor Wilks would philosophize in his portrait of *"Otumfuo Opoku Ware II as a Young Man,"* and which I borrow here, "He (Kufuor) spoke, emotionally, of those who had helped him, but who have now departed this life. It may have been his old friend, Victor Owusu or his revered mother, Ama Paa, but in remembering them, Kufuor wept. The tears were those of a man of strength, for only the weak cannot afford to cry." Saturday morning was the expected day for the Electoral Commissioner, to tell the nation at a press conference, the outcome of the results. When he did, after a winding speech, it became official.

"The final results of the December 28, 2000 elections," he said, were that, Kufuor had won with a 57 percent, three millions, six hundred and thirty-one thousand two hundred and sixty-three, of the votes. He had put up a good showing in all the regions of the country apart from the Volta region. He won 79 percent of votes in the Asante region, the NPP strongest base. Over 62 percent of votes in the Eastern region, 60 percent in the Central and Western regions, almost 60 percent in Greater Accra, 58 percent in Brong Ahafo and not less than 40 percent in the other regions registering. His lowest votes were in the

Volta region where he had only 11 percent.

At 3 p.m. on Saturday December 30, the President-elect John Agyekum Kufuor, dressed in an overall white with Mrs. Kufuor also in a white dress, symbolizing victory, a new life, a new era and with a heavy security presence in his house where the flag of Ghana and the colours of the nation—red, gold and green were already on display, gave a press conference to a riveting crowd.

I would like to express my thanks to God for all he has done for me.

I would like to thank all Ghanaians. Your faith in multi-party democracy, your patience and fortitude in the face of many challenges have brought us here to this momentous day.

I would like to thank my entire family, especially my wife, Theresa, for the support I have enjoyed from them in the struggle.

To my fellow party members who have toiled for so long without reward, driven on by their faith in the ideals, I say 'Ayekoo'. To Dr. Edward Mahama, Professor George Hagan, Mr. Goosie Tandoh, Dr. Wereko Brobby and Mr. Dan Lartey, the leaders, members and supporters of The People's National Convention, The Convention People's Party, The National Reform Party, The United Ghana Movement and The Great Consolidated People's Party, I say a big thank you for your active and highly effective support.

I would like to thank our foreign friends and donors who have stood by Ghana over these many years. I hope and trust that Ghana can continue to count on your understanding and support in the months and years to come, as we seek to deepen our democratic roots and tackle the tremendous problems that face our nation.

To the Chairman of the Electoral Commission, the members of the Commission and the staff, I say well done. I hope that the problems encountered in the December 28 run-off election will form a basis for continuous improvement in our electoral process.

I would also wish to thank all our security and civil servants. We are well aware and appreciative of the contributions you continue to make to Ghana. Let me restate once more that everybody has his or her part to play in my administration; there will be no room for witch-hunting of individuals or groups.

We have to look forward and concentrate on building our nation. I ask for your loyal support and help to make the transition from the out-going Government to the new administration as easy and as productive as possible.

And finally, I would like to thank His Excellency the Vice President, John Atta Mills, for his gracious concession. My thanks also go to His Excellency President Rawlings, who at the end of his mandated term under the democratic Constitution, has presided over this historic election.

I reiterate my intention to accord President Rawlings all the respect and support that is due to an ex-Head of State. I will ensure that he is treated, as I would like to be treated at the end of my term of office.

Yesterday, I was the candidate of my party, the New Patriotic Party. Today, thanks to the votes of so many millions of our citizens, am the President, not of the New Patriotic Party, but of all Ghanaians.

I pledge to be always mindful of this and to work as hard as I can each and everyday, to bring about a positive change in the lives of all our people. Fellow Ghanaians, for the first time in our history, we have voted one Government out of office and voted an infant one to replace it. This is a real achievement for our infant democracy and we deserve all the congratulations we give each other. However, even as we pat ourselves on the back, we must remain mindful that this is only the beginning.

Ahead of us lies the challenge of our deteriorating economy, our depreciating currency and other problems of which we are all aware.

We must now together take hold of the challenges that face our country and resolve to solve them in a spirit of unity, of reconciliation, of compassion and understanding. We must move forward into the new century as One Nation and One people with one manifest destiny.

In conclusion, I ask all of you for your prayers and support for the in-coming government and myself.

We are at the start of a brand new century and with your support we can work to make it the Ghanaian century. God bless Ghana, God bless us all. Thank you.

A journey no matter how long it takes must come to an end. Sometimes with many tales. Even Chaucer's literary ancient journey to Canterbury with the imaginary characters ended. It gave us *The Canterbury Tales*.

Kufuor's journey gave Ghana the third presidency of the Fourth Republic. On January 7, 2001, he was sworn in as such. Thousands of peoples from all over the country thronged to the Independence Square in Accra to see the new image for the new era. The singing and dancing signified nothing short of joy.

Expectations of what he could do, varied. To thousands of people, they were just happy to see a change of Government. To the generality of the people however, Kufuor, to remind us of the lyrics of the campaign song, was the man with the vision to rescue Ghana from oppression and suppression and also make the country a happy home.

Thus, he promised to show results in the four years of his presidency. At the close of the presidential ceremonies on January 7, the imagery that reinforced these feelings for him, was the thousands of peoples still singing and chasing his presidential car amidst tight security.

Their hopes—in the joy of the moment, were a reminder of his enormous responsibilities. "They have invested their hopes in me and I cannot fail them." Kufuor said upon reflection.

May God help his belief!

REVIEW AND PRAISE OF AUTHOR'S WORK.

Ivor Agyeman-Duah is well known internationally. In 1998-99, he held a research fellowship at the W.E.B. Du Bois Institute for Afro-American Studies at Harvard University, and has served as counselor and advisor to many scholars from the United States, Great Britain and elsewhere. He has devoted much time to the investigation of Ghana's past. He draws on extensive knowledge of orally transmitted materials, and interprets these with reference to evidence drawn from a broad range of documentary sources.

Between Faith and History—A Biography of J.A. Kufuor *follows this exemplary style. He thus exemplifies the ability to combine traditional and modern scholarship that was so characteristic of the seminal researches of his late and revered father, Joseph Agyeman-Duah.*

—Ivor Wilks,
Herskovits Professor Emeritus of African History,
Northwestern University, Evanston.

A good biography reveals not only the life of its subject but also the times in which the person lived. If the biography is of a politician, the book should encompass insights into the politics of the era. Ivor Agyeman-Duah's book about President J.A. Kufuor achieves that fusion of narrative between the biography of a man and the history of a country.

—Ali A. Mazrui,
Albert Schweitzer Professor in the Humanities,
State University of New York.

Mr. Agyeman-Duah has emerged from his early 20s into his mid 30s as one of the best literary writers in Ghana today. In several published works, he has sought to capture for posterity the rich history and traditions of Ghana. His epic TV documentary and companion book on the anti-colonial campaign of Yaa Asantewaa, the Queen of Ejisu reflects this.

He was the first Ghanaian journalist to literally predict in a 1994 article that J.A. Kufuor will be President one day. Anybody who wants to understand the contemporary politics of Ghana and Kufuor's role should read this new book, Between Faith and History—A Biography of J.A. Kufuor.

**—Kabral Blay Amihere,
Ghana's Ambassador to Sierra Leone and President Emeritus, West Africa Journalists Association.**

Mr. Agyeman-Duah is a very exciting media personality.

**—Ama Ata Aidoo,
Author of *Dilemma of a Ghost.***

Agyeman-Duah is one who will make things happen in the intellectual front in the coming years.

**—S.K.B. Asante,
President, Ghana Academy of Arts and Sciences.**

This narrative becomes more enjoyable if readers picture the actors in the context of other published works by the historian Paul Nugent in The Flight—Lieutenant and the Professor: The Road to Ghana's Fourth Republic, *and* Big Men, Small Boys and Politics in Ghana: Power, Ideology and the Burden of History: 1982-1994. *Certainly, these books will contribute to the discussion, especially regarding the pol-*

itics of the Fourth Republic.

—**Prof. David Owusu-Ansah,**
James Madison University, U.S.A.

Index

Dapaah, Nana Ama [Ama
Paa], 3, 4-6, 8, 12-13,21,
28,74
Denkyirahene, 3
Durowaa, Nana Akua, 5
Duodu, Rebecca, 6
Diawuo, Oyokohene
Kwapong, 7
Diawuo, Kofi, 7
Duah, Asantehene Kwaku, 9
Danquah, J.B., 11-13, 25, 32
Dyke, Charles Van, 26
Danquah-Busia Club
[Tradition], 50, 52-54,
56,60,63
Da Rocha, B. J. 60, 80, 86
Dagombas, 61
Darko, Kwabena, 66, 74
Donkor Fordwor, Kwame, 74,
75, 85
Deyaka, Salifu Bawa, 80
Databank Financial Services,
114

E
Ejisu-Asante [Juaben], 8, 81
Exeter College, 22, 24
Eyadema Gnassingbe, 47, 114
Ewe, 64
Electoral Commission
[National] 68, 93-
94,112,115,116,122
Erskine, Emmanuel, 66, 74
Essamuah, Colin, 74
Esseku, Haruna, 84
EGLE, 87, 108
Economic Commission of
West Africa States
[ECOWAS], 96, 110
Elizabeth II, Queen of
England, 110

'Esoho', 112
F
Fontomfrom, 7
Freeman, Thomas Birch, 9
Fuseni, A.B.A., 86
Freedom Forum, 115

G
Gold, 2-3, 108
Gold Coast, 2, 12, 22
Gyei, Kwadwo, 6
Gyamaduaa, Owusu, 9
Ghana Commercial Bank
[GCB], 28
Gbedema, Kobla Agbeli, 38
Ghandi, Indira, 40
Gyimah, A. Owusu, 50
Gyimah, Attakorah, 50
Ghana Academy of Arts and
Sciences [GAS], 61, 105
Gyasi, I.K., 77
Ghana Commission on
Human Rights [GCHR],
95
Ghana National Petroleum
Corporation [GNPC], 108
Garbrah, Ekow Spio, 110,
118
Gbagbo, Laurent, 114
Ghana Journalists Association
[GJA], 115
Ghana Broadcasting
Corporation [GBC], 115
Ghana International Press
Centre [GIPC], 116
Gyan, Afari, 117, 119

H
Hayford, Bentill Casely, 13
Hall, D.D., 23
Hansen, Johnny, 50